The Wardrobe Ensemble is a Bristol-based group of theatre artists working together to make and tour high-quality new plays that dissect the twenty-first-century experience. Dedicated to finding the place where the intellectual and the emotional collide, we explore the big ideas of our time through intimate human stories and bold imagery.

The Wardrobe Ensemble formed in 2011 out of the pilot year for Made in Bristol, Bristol Old Vic Young Company's graduate scheme for theatre companies. This was a one-year residency, where in exchange for leading and assisting workshops with the Young Company, we received training from various theatre practitioners and were given the space and time to make a show, *RIOT*, which we premiered in the Bristol Old Vic studio. We took *RIOT* to the Edinburgh Festival Fringe in 2011 and have been making work together ever since.

Our ensemble practice and politics inform the work we make and the stories we tell. Every company member has an equal voice in the artistic direction of the company and this ethos is reflected in the rehearsal room. We work as a democratic devising ensemble wherein every member contributes to the research, writing, structuring and performing of a show, creating a unique shared theatrical language and aesthetic from show to show. We create our work in dialogue with each other and then continue that conversation with our audience.

The company consists of nine core members, one producer and a constantly growing community of associate artists. We have made six full-company shows: *RIOT*, *33*, *1972: The Future of Sex*, *Education, Education, Education*, *South Western* and *The Last of the Pelican Daughters*, and nine shows for families and young audiences: *The Star Seekers*, *The Time Seekers*, *The Deep Sea Seekers*, *Eliza and the Wild Swans*, *Edgar and the*

Land of Lost, *Eloise and the Curse of the Golden Whisk*, *Little Tim and the Brave Sea Captain*, *The Forever Machine* and *The Wind in the Willows*.

We have toured our work nationally and internationally to venues including the National Theatre, Almeida Theatre, Exeter Northcott, Salisbury Playhouse, Theatre Royal Plymouth and Northern Stage. We have won two Stage Awards and a Fringe First. We are Complicité Associates and Associate Artists of The Wardrobe Theatre and Shoreditch Town Hall.

www.thewardrobeensemble.com

The Wardrobe Ensemble

THE LAST OF THE PELICAN DAUGHTERS

*A Wardrobe Ensemble, Complicité
and Royal & Derngate Northampton co-production,
in association with Bristol Old Vic and Pleasance*

NICK HERN BOOKS

London

www.nickhernbooks.co.uk

A Nick Hern Book

The Last of the Pelican Daughters first published in Great Britain in 2020 as a paperback original by Nick Hern Books Limited, The Glasshouse, 49a Goldhawk Road, London W12 8QP, in association with The Wardrobe Ensemble

The Last of the Pelican Daughters copyright © 2020 The Wardrobe Ensemble

The Wardrobe Ensemble have asserted their moral right to be identified as the authors of this work

Extract from 'This Be The Verse' © the Estate of Philip Larkin, first published in *High Windows*. Reproduced by permission of Faber & Faber Ltd

Cover photos: front © Graeme Braidwood; inside front © James Bullimore

Designed and typeset by Nick Hern Books, London
Printed in the UK by Mimeo Ltd, Huntingdon, Cambridgeshire PE29 6XX

A CIP catalogue record for this book is available from the British Library

ISBN 978 1 84842 935 2

Contents

Introduction

by Tom Brennan and Jesse Jones, co-directors

When we met with Judith Dimant of Complicité (and now Wayward Productions) in 2016, she said that we reminded her of a young Complicité (which is always exactly what an emerging theatre company wants to hear). As much as this was to do with theatrical style, it was perhaps more to do with the non-hierarchical form of our company, and the intensity of the relationships between company members. We're a tight-knit group with our own traditions, secrets and mythologies, crafted over the decade we've spent working together. (Some of the important shifts and changes in our story are documented in the oral history which follows this note.) In that meeting, she asked us if there was a show that we wanted to make, but were too terrified and felt too inexperienced to do so.

We'd been speaking about making The Wardrobe Ensemble's version of a 'family drama' for some years. As much as we loved watching stories about families, from Greek tragedy to *The Simpsons*, it felt like so much of what we associated with 'family drama' was formally stuck within a kind of naturalism that didn't reflect our tastes or theatrical sensibilities. On top of this, the most famous works of family drama explored the particular quirks and traumas of a singular playwright. Tennessee Williams' 'memory' play *The Glass Menagerie*, for example, reads like a therapy session for the writer. Would it be possible for a group rather than a single writer, or more importantly *our* group, with our particular quirks and differences of experience to embark on such a therapy/creation experience? How would we excavate and interrogate our collective familial demons? Is there anything to be revealed about our time and generation? Importantly in those early conversations, we were sure that our show would look nothing like a family drama that you've seen before. It would mess with the conventions of the genre and reflect our own world-view and style. Judith liked this idea the best.

Somewhat ironically, but perhaps tellingly, what emerged is the most naturalistic play that we've ever made, one that adheres to many narrative and stylistic conventions of 'traditional' or 'straight' plays of the past. It's got plenty more silence, subtext and emotional performance than any of our other work. Similarly, the themes and characters look and sound like plays of the past: it begins with a death, it's about a house, someone is having a baby. There's more than a hint of *The Cherry Orchard*'s Varya in Storm, or the ghost of King Hamlet in Rosemary Pelican. And it's important to say that all of this convention felt terrifying for us. Making a 'proper' play felt extremely difficult. Naturalism felt unnatural.

So much of devising lies in an ability to give up certain aspects of control and let a show emerge. The work that comes out of us collectively is not driven by a singular voice, but emerges through the collective character of the company. And so, it's weird that we made this. This isn't the show that any one of us wanted to make. But despite our best efforts, it's the show that the company needed to make.

We understood that to deconstruct a family drama we needed to make one. But by the time we built one that functioned – designed the family, found their stories and struggles, built the pink house, etc. – deconstructing them all felt like a disingenuous act. Though we often felt embarrassed by their behaviour and the interpersonal issues that were emerging in the play, we did care about the Pelicans. We had to, because to varying degrees, their stories are our stories. And that isn't to say that we have undying love and affection for these characters. Ask any member of the company about how much irony is in the play, and it will differ. Some will say 'This is my family', some will say 'I fucking hate these privileged arseholes', and some will acknowledge what is maybe closest to the truth: 'This is a version of The Wardrobe Ensemble.'

We tried to make the show flashier, cooler and more energetic. We tried to make the characters address their political context more directly, as we might have done in previous work. But these attempts felt dishonest. Perhaps because we were all in a process of grappling with an ugly truth, that we were starting to care about so-called 'grown-up things'. Our work used to explore the world in hypothetical or nostalgic terms, but what do we *actually* worry about now? What keeps us up at night are often the same questions that are affecting the Pelican children: What do I want my life to look like? What do I need to get there? How long can I exist in this chaotic ensemble? Do I always have to share? What kind of an adult do I want to be?

In March this year (2020), we remounted this show in Northampton ready for our UK tour. After a few rewrites and additions, and a partial re-cast (the wonderful Sally Cheng, Laurie Jamieson and Bea Scirocchi joined the team), the show was ready to hit the road. We were struck by how much more comfortable we had become with *The Last of the Pelican Daughters*. We were able to lean into the naturalism, pace and emotion of it with far more confidence. It seemed we had finally accepted the strange thing we had collectively given birth to. Had we become what we sought to reject? Had we actually become adults? And then, of course, COVID-19. We were at the Nuffield in Southampton (NST) when it was announced the government strongly advised the public not to go to theatres any more. The tour was cancelled and all the professional stability that we had tried so hard to build over the past ten years had disappeared overnight. We dismantled the set and packed it away. NST has since gone into administration. And so, as we write this (in early July), we find ourselves reflecting on the show in vastly different ways.

If this play is our first reckoning with the proper realities of being grown-ups, there are two diametrically opposing messages that the show seems to reflect back at us.

Firstly, that our mission of collective theatre-making and non-hierarchical structures was naive and hypocritical. Instead, we should have cared about real 'adult things'. The Pelican children lose their house and their inheritance at the end of the play, because at some level, they just weren't paying attention. From one perspective, we as a company have buried our heads in the sand for the last ten years. We've been making financially unsustainable choices since day one. So perhaps it's time to kill the dream and start making responsible choices. Maybe the Tories are right. Maybe we should wake up to the reality that we live in a capitalist society before we lose everything we hold dear.

But secondly, that dramatic changes to our reality can come out of nowhere, whether you've behaved like an 'adult' or not. Susie Stephens of Stephen Stephens and Sons Solicitors will always interrupt breakfast. And so, now more than ever, it feels vital that we hold onto the families that we find ourselves in. The idealism of Rosemary Pelican and indeed The Wardrobe Ensemble is unrealistic, but at the moment we're not sure what isn't. As the coronavirus leaves our world's safety, economy and future on shaky ground, we need communities, rituals, traditions, secrets and mythologies to hold onto more than ever. And if we really are the grown-ups now, it's our responsibility to define the culture of the families in which we exist. It's up to us to choose what to bring forward into the future and what to abandon. It's our responsibility to start building a house in which we actually want to live.

The Pelican Daughters set on stage at Nuffield Southampton Theatres before we had to take it all down again (photo: Tom Crosley-Thorne).

The Wardrobe Ensemble meeting on Zoom (photo: Tom Brennan).

An Oral History of The Wardrobe Ensemble

The birth of the company happened on a training programme called Made in Bristol – still running today. Before this, some of us had worked together on shows at the Bristol Old Vic Young Company. Some of us had never met before. *Emily Greenslade, member of TWE*

We rehearsed in a stark empty room with broken tiles that used to be BOV's Wardrobe department. We decided to call ourselves The Wardrobe Ensemble. The first thing we ever agreed on. *James Newton, member of TWE*

One of the recurring themes early on in our company's history was blazing rows. Creative, professional, personal, you name it; we argued, we cried, we made each other cry, we shouted and we blamed. But despite all the tears there were always glimmers of reconciliation, of apologies and of 'talking things out'. This culture of 'debriefing' as we called it, started informally but increasingly became an important part of the emotional and logistical backbone of the company. *Ben Vardy, member of TWE*

RIOT

We made our first show, *RIOT*, about a riot in an unnamed Swedish furniture store. It went much better than we thought it would. At a special performance for some delegates from other youth theatre organisations, a gruff, no-nonsense Northern man asked what we thought was good about the play. We replied with some sincere bullshit: 'the ensemble', 'the energy', the commitment'. 'No,' he said, 'the play's alright. It's the idea that's good.' We didn't really get it at the time. I think we're only just beginning to now. We're very lucky that we have 'ideas people' in the company. People who instinctively know what constitutes a good idea and come up with lots of them (I am not one of those people). *James*

Tom and I pitched for £500 from the National Student Drama Festival to help fund *RIOT* in Edinburgh. It went well and they seemed to like the idea of the show. They did not give us the £500 but they did give us some very sound legal advice to stop us getting sued by IKEA. *Jesse Jones, member of TWE*

We took *RIOT* to Edinburgh. We put bets on who would have a fight. After our first performance to a silent audience who looked like they'd rather be anywhere else, we resigned to the fact that 'it obviously just isn't a good show'. *Jesse Meadows, member of TWE*

For a totally new company we had a good crowd of around fifteen people. People were bored, someone left, no one laughed. We did more rehearsals that night and wrote a new monologue to open the show. But that night when we went to bed, the London riots kicked off. Suddenly, our little show felt like the most pertinent and political thing out there. We sold out the run. It changed from a physical comedy to a biting satire without us doing anything. It was a big lesson in the power of context. *Tom Brennan, member of TWE*

Facebook took down our Facebook event, called '*RIOT* in Edinburgh' for inciting violence. We got a full-page spread in the *Edinburgh Evening Post*. *James*

After that, it was a whirlwind month. We would scream whenever we received a good review and all gather in the living room with me reading it aloud from the top of a chair. *Jesse M*

Tom's grandmother was convinced that I really did have a jaguar tattoo on my bum (as my character Nicki declares) and she still swears that she's seen it! I think I should probably get one, just to prove her right. *Edythe Woolley, member of TWE*

We washed our costumes twice that month. I smelled smells I'd never smelled before. *James*

Extract from Tom Brennan's Edinburgh blog
And so our Edinburgh adventures have begun. There is a LOT of crazy stuff going on as you can imagine. We ain't in Kansas any more. Our advertising onslaught is going incredibly well. The supreme charm of Jesse Jones has done us proud. Also,

we've been attaching tags to things all over the city: trees, rails, toilets, chairs, handles, etc. Some have been ripped off, some have got us in trouble from venues, and some have got us some real attention from the punters. We've also been fighting each other on the [Royal] Mile. *Tom B*

On the way home, the rest of the company got off the train in Bristol while I stayed on to Yatton. Everyone sang to me from the platform, and I cried. That first Edinburgh was one big, magical dream, and I don't think I'll ever quite have that feeling again. *James*

There's been moments in the company history that have been real turning points. 'Make or break' if you like. The most significant perhaps took place in the tiny Soho Theatre green room in September 2011. We'd been invited to do a week of performances there as part of 'The Best of the Fringe'. After the last show we gathered there deciding what to do about this company we'd just formed, this show we'd just made, when half the members were about to continue onto higher education. The other half of us had just graduated. We had a vote about the future and decided to attempt a tour and recast the people who wouldn't be able to do it. We could have easily called it a wonderful experience and had done with it, but the magic of the last month was somehow holding us together. Something was telling us to keep going. So I created a spreadsheet of small-scale theatres, made a tour pack and sent off emails. Ben and Jones then followed each up with a phone call. And by the end of it we had our first little tour booked. And it wasn't even that little. We ordered all the flyers to Bristol, counted them out, packaged them up and sent them to every venue. We had no funding. Just a lot of Young Persons Railcards and a car full of IKEA lamps. *Jesse M*

Before each performance I'd get out the iron and iron all our Primark 'IKEA' shirts with Kerry. We were the tour washer-folks. *Edythe*

After our Edinburgh success, I remember not understanding why theatres weren't throwing commissioning money at us. I thought we were the best. But we had just made one show. *Tom B*

The next three years saw me squeezing TWE stuff into every holiday I had. The already graduated side of the company kept the ship running, touring *RIOT* for peanuts and making our first family work. It must have been bloody tough, and I'll always be grateful for them keeping the engine running. *James*

We start meeting every week on Skype. And so begins the long, arduous and important process of running a company together, as democratically as possible. People working in the industry who are far older and more experienced tell us over and over that our model of working doesn't make any sense. That we need to make a company with fewer people. *Tom B*

We've met online every Monday evening for the last nine years. Thank you, technology. *Jesse M*

I came into the Wardrobe family part way through the story, a new addition a couple of years into their journey. I stepped in for Ben playing the role of James Blumpt in a remount of *RIOT* back in 2012 in the old Bristol Old Vic Studio. We had a short week to rehearse, before performing a handful of shows over a weekend. Almost immediately I felt completely at home in the group. I had known a good number of them for years, as part of the Bristol Old Vic Young Company and already shared a similar understanding of making work. I'd known Jimmy as a chubby young teen, performed alongside Kerry in *Samson and Delilah*, Meadows in *Blood Wedding*, and looked up to many others in the company. I remember being so excited coming into rehearsals for that week. I was so impressed by what they had already achieved, even at that early stage. The fact they had devised and written their own show was, to 21-year-old Tom England just out of university, an absolute marvel. I just wanted to impress them. Which I'm sure they will find laughable now. To think that I was nervous working with them all. To think I saw this as a big break for me. But it was. It really felt that way. It felt like an opportunity to show my friends that I could work with them well and could bring a good vibe and energy to the room. I hope I did, and continue to do so. *Tom England, Associate Artist*

We've been to so many places. We've performed to one person and we've performed to 1000 people. I think the weirdest ones are the best ones. They stay with you. On our first ever tour of *RIOT* we performed to twelve people in a carpeted conference room complete with fireplace and house plants. We've performed in tents, and classrooms, and lecture theatres. Town halls, and proscenium-arch auditoriums and studios made of tin foil. *Kerry Lovell, member of TWE*

When we performed *RIOT* at the Edinburgh Fringe, unbeknownst to us, it was seen by Sara Katzoff and Peter Wise, two people in charge of running a small theatre festival in the Berkshires, Massachusetts. They invited us to that festival, and despite the fact that we were very poor and very inexperienced, we looked at each other and realised we couldn't say no. We all had to apply for visas and so we learned each other's middle names. Benjamin Gideon Vardy is a good one. I made all the girls a snack pack for the plane, we travelled across the ocean together for the first time. At the end of each performance in America we got Jimmy (because he's got a nice face) to stand with a donation hat. Someone gave us a $100 bill – good job, Jimmy. Edie drove us all around in a rusty, stinky car which we all piled into – it gets nicknamed 'The Clown Car'. We do a one-off performance in New York City – our amp breaks and we make all the sound with our mouths, it is messy and stressful and exhilarating. Afterwards, we eat pizza sat on a rooftop overlooking the city skyline. Kerry and I have a little moment – overwhelmed, emotional, happy. *Helena Middleton, member of TWE*

It was an amazing festival and we had the best fun that summer. In those days, we had a terrifying wildness of spirit. We were inseparable. We spent our time drinking, dancing, swimming in the lake and *trying* to develop our next show. We only ate corn on the cob because it was the only cheap thing we could find in the shops. We were full of in-jokes and competitive games. Someone (JJ) decided that we weren't allowed to go to bed before a certain hour of the morning. So I remember Jesse literally dragging Jimmy out of bed and back into the party. One afternoon, we tried to play a party game with the staff of the festival, and we got so competitive and angry at each other that we had to stop playing and be separated into different rooms. I bet we were absolutely obnoxious company. *Tom B*

Half of us were under twenty-one, which meant legally we weren't supposed to go out. But we sneakily discovered that our regular UK driving licences worked! Confused by the month and date reversal that happens in the US, bouncers clocked that our date of birth was vaguely intact so they just let us in. Perfect. *Edythe*

Jimmy, Edie and I flying to New York on Jimmy's birthday will always hold a special place in my heart. We went up the Empire State, and although we could not see anything for the rain clouds, we had a great time imagining how long our poos would take to reach the ground floor once flushed in the toilet at the top. Other things that happened in New York that trip include a great night in a comedy club, having no power in a show of *RIOT*, and for the first time me threatening to get a coat-hanger tattoo. *Jesse J*

A highlight of the Berkshire Fringe was meeting Hector and Chloe who worked at the festival. They were very cool, beautiful queer people that entered our lives whom I am forever grateful for and hold fondly in my heart, although we have lost touch now. Once a week Hector and Chloe would take some of us on the three-hour drive from Massachusetts to Queens NYC to the lesbian bar Bum Bum Bar (said like Boom Boom) for the drag nights. It was popping! We stayed for the shows and the cheap cocktails and danced salsa real close, sweating with the dykes and queens in the little basement room. It was perfect. For most of us it was our first truly queer-clubbing experience. We made the journey every week for the next month, driving home at the end of the night to get a few winks of sleep and then straight back to rehearsals the following day (only something you can do in your early twenties!). We were in the very early stages of devising *33*, working on epic fight sequences, choreography and romcom scenes between washed-up news reporters, made all the more hilarious by the lack of sleep. The exhaustion was totally worth it. I was playing Elvis Presley at the time – I suppose it was the first time I did drag. Bum Bum Bar sadly closed in 2018 and now there are only three lesbian bars left in NYC. *Edythe*

After *RIOT*, we were invited for a meeting at the National with a man we have a lot to thank for: Sebastian Born. They wanted to support the development of our second show and we were discussing ideas. During this meeting he gave me one of the best pieces of advice we've received: 'Whatever happens, make sure you make a *third* show.' He didn't know at that moment how much we needed to hear that. Our second show, *33*, was a tough learning curve and it was indeed our third which was a lot easier and proved in many ways our 'break-though show'. Thanks Bash! *Jesse M*

33

We managed to wangle a week's R&D for *33*, which was about the 2010 Chilean mining disaster, at the National Theatre Studio. We couldn't believe our eyes when we walked in. It was so big! And so bright! The ceilings were so high! Lots of famous people had been here! We stuck up our research with Blu Tack and ruined the walls. *James*

At one point we figured out that we needed a producer. A meeting was organised in London with Marianne Dicker, who worked at the National Theatre. Marianne was going to give us advice on finding a producer. As the only member of the company that lived in London at the time, it was decided that I should go. The main thing I remember from that discussion is that she said, 'You can either get an older, highly experienced producer who will have industry connections but you'd be just one of their many clients. Or, you could find a producer your age, with less experience but they would grow with you and could focus more fully on the company.' The second one sounded more exciting, and I asked if she could recommend anyone. 'I'd like you to meet someone called Hannah Smith.' A few weeks later, again as the only Londoner, I was asked to go and meet the elusive Hannah Smith in Covent Garden over 'Tea and Biscuits', despite the fact that I've never liked drinking tea, but I comforted myself with the prospect of the biscuits. Hannah seemed wise, funny and very interested in our company, and so I invited her to come and see the work-in-progress performance of our next show, *33*. *Ben*

I knew Marianne because she had interviewed me for a job at the National Theatre that I didn't get. I was so upset not to get it that I cried down the phone to the poor HR man who had to break the news. But somehow, indirectly, it led to a job that I've now had for nearly eight years and that I can't really imagine my life without. *Hannah Smith, Producer*

We did a showing of *33* in Bristol. We invited every important person we could think of and, surprisingly, many came. We kicked off the sharing with 'Occasionally', a complex, overlapping, ensemble musical number sung and played entirely by the cast. The only problem is, we couldn't really sing and most of us had never picked up the instrument we were playing before the start of that week. It was a disaster, our first proper experience of failure. That scar will forever be etched into our company's collective psyche. *James*

I directed *33*, and I watched the special work-in-progress sharing at Bristol Old Vic. It wasn't that bad. *Tom B*

Amazingly, that was the first time Hannah saw our work and she still agreed to produce us. She says it was good, but I do question her taste sometimes (she's my girlfriend now). *James*

I was liaising with Hannah about her visit to watch our showing of *33*. We'd never met before and I said she'd be fine to stay over at mine. On the day, my housemate retracted the offer to borrow his bed, so Hannah and I snuggled into my small double bed which only just fit my tiny bedroom. I felt so embarrassed and was sure this wasn't how a professional relationship was meant to start, but she didn't seem bothered and as we stayed up chatting I had a feeling maybe she didn't think we were totally weird. We've consequently spent the next seven years sharing beds. *Jesse M*

We made *33* in 'the hut' in Bath. We were doing 10 a.m. to 10 p.m. days as we could only afford a couple of weeks of rehearsals. After that process we vowed never to work twelve hours straight again on the trot. It was so so hot in that hut, I'm half-convinced it was a greenhouse! We had to strip down to our underwear to rehearse. *Edythe*

We took it to Edinburgh. The only slot available was really late which meant the Military Tattoo happened at the end of our show every night. You could hear gunfire and cannons over the top of Kerry's final monologue. *Ben*

Once when I was flyering I said, 'A show about the Chilean miners' – and a man just shouted, 'WHY?!' *Helena*

33 in Edinburgh was tough for lots of the company but to be honest, apart from having to operate the first show with no lighting cues in the desk as they hadn't saved from our tech, I had a great time. It was my only Edinburgh as a singleton, I was being paid by the National Theatre as I had just started a job there, I made loads of new friends, I went out till very late very regularly, I watched a man split a watermelon on his head, threatened to get a coat-hanger tattoo and ate loads of McDonald's... What more do you want? *Jesse J*

I was asked to step in for Jimmy when *33* went on tour in 2013. I donned his well-worn boiler suit, and stepped into his shoes as Edison Pena. I think, for some in the company, *33* felt like a bit of a tough nut to crack. They will often jokingly refer to it as a 'tricky second album'. To me, once again treading the line between insider and outsider, it felt like a genuine accomplishment. It was a bold and technically challenging piece of work. Looking back, I view that tour through an incredibly positive lens. Despite one or two personal and professional hiccups, the tour was a success. It was an opportunity to learn more, to hone my craft as an ensemble performer working alongside some of my childhood friends. It was also the first time I had committed myself fully to theatre as a professional endeavour. *Tom E*

I wasn't in the tour of *33*, so I went to see it at Battersea Arts Centre. The first time I'd actually watched any of our work. I hated it, and I was very bad at hiding it afterwards. I don't think they've ever really forgiven me for that. *James*

The Bike Shed

We make three Christmas shows for the Bike Shed Theatre in Exeter. The titles get progressively weirder: *Eliza and the Wild Swans*, *Edgar and the Land of Lost* and *Eloise and the Curse of the Golden Whisk*. We meet Hannah Kamen when we make *Edgar and The Land of Lost*. She becomes a regular collaborator and Associate Artist. She's amazing. We love her. Emily and I are the only members of the company to perform in the show so we spend the season together. We live in a lovely older couple's house with their slobbery old dog. On New Year's Eve, Emily and I snog. What a cliché! *Tom B*

After uni I had moved to Berlin with my then-girlfriend, Anne. I worked as a waiter. I watched no theatre (amazing). I learned German. While I was there, Tom and Em got into a relationship. Tom didn't tell me, and that really upset me. *James*

When rehearsing *Edgar and the Land of Lost* in a shop-front rehearsal room in Exeter I was staying in digs and thanks to a key mix-up found myself locked out for the night, walking around the streets of Exeter alone. I realised that I did have the keys to the rehearsal room so I went and slept in there and didn't tell anyone for a long time. I also think I still managed to be late to rehearsals that day. *Jesse J*

Eloise and the Curse of the Golden Whisk. One month rehearsing and one month performing in a damp, dingy cellar in Exeter. The schedule was punishing, I sweated a lot, we all got ill. But it was paid work. Solid, paid work. I worked hard. I loved it. *James*

Jesse Meadows and I not only shared a room but also a double bed for two months in Exeter while we were making and performing *Eloise*. Everyone was bunking-up, squeezing into small spaces that had been gifted to us and making do with what we had as we had very little income at this point and no company money-pot. *Edythe*

Whilst making *Eloise* we listened to the *Monsters University* soundtrack on repeat and danced our hearts out up and down the streets of Exeter. David Lockwood who ran The Bike Shed was an incredible support in our early years. He brought his son

Ludo into rehearsals when he was a mere two days old and we all had a hold. He even let us put him in a saucepan on stage. *Jesse M*

The Bike Shed closed in 2018 and we made *The Wardrobe Ensemb-Wheel of Fortune* to celebrate its last weekend. A compilation of loads of TV game shows, including *Hole in the Wall*, it's probably the silliest thing we've ever done. *Hannah*

Extract from our post to The Bike Shed on its closing day
To The Bike Shed – thank you for taking a punt on a company that was barely two years old, and agreeing to let us make your Christmas show, *Eliza and the Wild Swans*. This decision is almost entirely responsible for kickstarting our entire strand of family work, and we don't underestimate how much of a risk that must have been for you. Thank you for teaching us that it isn't always easy, but it's always worth it in the end. *TWE*

The Star Seekers

When someone asks about The Wardrobe Ensemble's journey I often talk about how much we said 'Yes' in those first, formative years. 'Should we take our first show to Edinburgh, we'll need to somehow raise £5000' – 'Yes!'... 'Should we take that same show to America, borrow a rickety car that smells like rat wee and try not to starve' – 'Yes!'... 'Should we make another show, and another, and another' – 'Yes, yes, yes!' This mildly foolish but totally glorious yay-saying was what led us to make our first show for younger years. The Wardrobe Theatre had £500 from the Bristol Council to spend on a kids' show and asked if we wanted to make it and we, of course, said 'Yes!' And so we made *The Star Seekers* – an interactive space adventure for 3 to 8-year-olds – in a room above a pub in Bristol. *Helena*

We created the set from things we found in skips and sprayed silver. I asked a new friend, Nicola Holter, to make us costumes as a favour. She said yes! She has since designed all of our *Seekers* shows – and her, Helena and I now live together. *Jesse M*

We have now toured *The Star Seekers* and its follow-up show *The Time Seekers* all over the country, to schools, festivals, theatres and town halls. I directed the shows but I am also the technician and so I have seen these shows hundreds of times and genuinely, each show is joyful because it is always original. That is because of the kids in the audience. I've seen a dinosaur playing hide and seek, I've seen an alien made of pants digging up rocks on its planet to find ice cream, I've seen an audience perform surgery on a black hole.

We also said 'Yes' to taking *The Star Seekers* to Edinburgh in 2017 to play alongside our full-company adult show *Education, Education, Education*. Whilst *EEE* was selling out, we were really struggling to get an audience to come to *TSS*, as the competition was large, established, known-title children's shows. Whilst the rest of The Wardrobe Ensemble were collecting our Fringe First for *EEE*, we performed *The Star Seekers* to six people, of which only two were children, but amongst those watching was someone from the outreach department at the National Theatre. The show then got programmed to play for a month at the Dorfman in summer 2018. You never know what might lead to what. *Helena*

1972: The Future of Sex

1972: The Future of Sex, or at that time known as 'The History of Fucking'. Our third full-company show. We started with a two-week development process at Shoreditch Town Hall. This was a big moment. The second half of the group had just graduated from university so it was the first time we were working together outside 'holidays'. *Jesse M*

This was a show about sex, relationships, gender and equality, all placed in a time we'd only heard cool things about: the '70s. This was a show that saw us trying to grapple with our place in the world and how that place was different from our parents. We were young, some of us only recently graduated, so figuring out who we were and how we wanted to be with each other seemed to be what we wanted to talk about. It contained big political ideas distilled into the most personal and intimate. *Emily*

We got our first ever Arts Council grant for the R&D. The letter arrived at my mum's house. She rang me to tell me while I was on an eight-hour Megabus to Manchester. I was absolutely ecstatic. *James*

Shoreditch Town Hall gave us some commission money after the first sharing. Discussing it beforehand we thought they might give us a couple of grand and then they offered five grand. We went to the pub and began to think that we could actually make this show happen and we could actually pay people. *Hannah*

For the first time we had all the time in the world. I flew back and forth from Berlin to help make *1972: The Future of Sex* in the basement of Shoreditch Town Hall. Perhaps it was the excitement of all the new possibilities that now lay before us; maybe it was the pocketful of new exercises and theories of the newly graduated; maybe it's just very easy and fun to talk about sex, but that creation process will always hold a special place in my heart. *James*

For me, I think this is the moment where I discovered that this was my job, no longer a hobby. We were still a bunch of kids playing but playing with support and a bit more seriousness. *Emily*

In our first few shows we felt like we could do it all. *We* played the instruments, *we* did the lights, *we* designed the show ourselves. This was born of necessity, but also spoke of our, at times, unhinged capacity to say, 'I can do that.' When we made *1972: The Future of Sex*, however, we enlisted experts for the first time. My friend Tom Crosely-Thorne (who I was in a band with as a teenager) wrote and played the most funkalicious music for the show, and Georgia Coleman (a close friend of Edie) designed a simple but glorious set. It lifted us up in so many ways. *Tom B*

Tom England joined us as a deviser (rather than a member of the touring cast) for the first time. I was in a young company show with him when I was 16 and he was 18. When I told my mum, her response was 'Oh that's lovely, you used to really admire him.' *James*

Making *1972* it really felt like we were both trying to make a show, and grapple with what kinds of people we wanted to be moving into adulthood, at least it did for me. It felt like a sort of coming-of-age process. The show, for anybody who hasn't seen it, was focused on gender and sexuality, reflecting on whether or not progress has been made since the 1970s in relation to those notions. As we made the show we reflected, often after rehearsals as we shared a drink together, on the way we make our work, the gendered dynamic in the room and the balance of voices. We came to realise that, more often than not, the male voices were the dominant ones in the room, in both conversation and in the creation of content. We worked hard to address that as best as we could during the rehearsals and it has informed the way we work together and communicate as a group ever since. Making *1972* had a massive impact on me personally. It really opened my eyes to things that I hadn't been able to see before. To hear friends of mine speak about their experience of their gender and how that has impacted the way they move, talk and react in the world was really eye-opening. It feels a bit silly to say this for some reason, but it helped me to become more empathetic I think. *Tom E*

This conversation had begun a few years ago when we took *RIOT* to The Shed at the National. Conversations around the patriarchy and how it plays out in our rehearsal room are challenging and emotional, but it was a really pivotal moment for us and it started a very important open dialogue about gender-based power structures and how we need to consciously work at not replicating them. It's a conversation that we continue to have to this day and which reflects gender issues in the industry. *Edythe*

We are a democracy, we make collaboratively, our shows are our shows because of the alchemy of having these exact people in the room. If one piece were different, the sliding door would close and the show would be totally different. At one point it felt as though the quieter voices were being overlooked, sometimes this was gendered, we had to work to boost those voices and encourage others to listen. But I want to caveat that with this: talent does not have to be loud, talent can be focused and attentive and collaborative. We are a stronger company because of what we each bring to the room. *Helena*

One day, Tom (Brennan) joked that he would love to see me naked onstage with my willy tucked between my legs, doing Renaissance poses. I've now done exactly that for thousands of people (including family, friends, parents of friends and old teachers). The best ideas often pretend that they're jokes. *James*

We didn't get our second Art Council application for *1972* but decided to do it anyway. We cut our own wages and wallpapered the set ourselves. *Hannah*

We took it to Edinburgh. It was our 'breakout show'. We were reviewed by the critic Lyn Gardner for the first time. I remember the feeling when I clocked her blonde hair in the audience – a feeling many people in our world have experienced. *James*

Edinburgh that year was hilarious. The show was received really well and we had the time of our lives. Somehow we volunteered ourselves to run a late-night chat-show sort of thing called *Down to Funk* whereby Kerry and Ben Vardy were the hosts of a madcap show a bit like a late-night *This Morning*. Ben in his element, Kerry decidedly out of her comfort zone but keeping things running smoothly as she always does. We performed *Down to Funk* in the small bar/café space at ZOO venues. I say performed, more fumbled I'd say. We fumbled and stumbled through two hours of craziness. Me pretending to be a Mr Motivator-esque character called Tim Treadmill, Jimmy and Tom Brennan a pair of… well, I'm not sure exactly. I guess, sort of, weathermen? Also called Tim and Tim. Surprisingly, it was quite a niche hit with the crowds who turned out. *Tom E*

Extract from Jesse Meadows' Edinburgh blog
Every day of the show whilst we are waiting backstage as the audience comes in, we go round the circle, each giving our 'words of wisdom' for that day's performance. Usually different ways (some more ironic than others) of expressing our love for each other and for the show. Tom England used the Hawaiian word 'Ohana' – it means family. But more than family. The

extended sense of the word. Who are bound together. Who breathe together. I can honestly say my favourite moment of the day is performing the play. I wake up every morning looking forward to 4 p.m. – show time! And that is a very exciting feeling. *Jesse M*

We won the Stage Award for acting excellence that year, and the prestigious Mervyn Stutter's Pick of the Fringe. As we were presented with our Stage Award, the photographer, who up until then had kept himself hidden inconspicuously amongst the audience, came tumbling onto the stage as he tripped on some wiring. Poor bloke. He styled it out with aplomb though to be fair, a diving slide into gambol and standing with a flourish. Ten points. All the best. *Tom E*

We saw *The Encounter* by Complicité. We all thought it was the best thing we had ever seen. The second thing we ever agreed on. *James*

We flyered. We postered. We tweeted. We WhatsApped. We waved at each other across the road whilst flyering. We got well pissed out of our noggins. We waited every day on the stairs at 3.45 p.m. listening out for the exit music to *Miss Sarah*. Tom and Hannah sat on the stairs every day whilst we were getting into costume, lovingly putting flyers into programmes. Our techie Charlotte did super well on her A-levels. We spent a lot of time in ZOO Cab Bar. Jimmy and Ben cried into each other's arms at Jack Rooke's show *Good Grief*. We ironed *1972* transfers onto T-shirts. And then never wore them. *Jesse M*

I was there for the first five days and then went to London to rehearse another show. It was a vintage fringe for the company and it was hard not to be up in Scotland with the gang. I decided I would go up for the weekend at the end of the festival and booked some flights and an appointment at a tattoo parlour to finally get my coat-hanger tattoo. I missed my flight and my tattoo appointment. *Jesse J*

We took the show to Bestival. As I stood naked and vulnerable onstage, a drunk man strolled into the auditorium and yelled, 'WHAT THE HELL IS GOING ON HERE?!' It was hilarious. *James*

At the Bestival closing party, me and Han watched Kerry and Tom Crosley-Thorne share their first kiss in the rain. We loved it. They're still a couple. *James*

We performed *1972* at Shambala in the summer of 2015 I think. Which was probably one of the best and worst experiences of my life. Whoever decided to programme us in the world's hottest tent on the final day of the festival clearly didn't have our best interests at heart. The evening before I had been feeling a little peaky so, on the advice of Jimmy, had taken to a box of Chardonnay to lift my spirits. You can always rely on Jimmy for some solid advice. Standing side of stage the day after, however, his advice felt, well, not really like very good advice at all. More sabotage I'd say. To be fair, he'd also done a pretty good job of sabotaging himself too so I let him off. *Tom E*

After four days straight of partying, I had a bathroom incident directly before going on stage. It was the biggest and most appreciative crowd we've ever had – nearly 1000 people! The single biggest adrenaline rush of my life. *James*

Hands down one of the most incredible moments of my life. We exited the stage unsure if our wet faces were down to sweating or weeping. *Kerry*

On the press night of *1972* in Shoreditch, the carpet started to move when the cast were running on it. I was a nervous wreck and not doing a particularly good job of hiding it. Hannah gave me a look as if to say 'Sort your life out.' It was, of course, fine. *Jesse J*

My abiding memory of the *1972* tour was performing at The Bike Shed in Exeter when a good number of the cast was struck down by a short illness. Diplomatically put, you might describe the illness as 'sickness from both ends'. Thankfully I wasn't knocked down by it. We didn't have any understudies at that time and we couldn't cancel any shows, so resourceful as we are, we just made do with a couple of old buckets in the dressing room. That's showbiz, kids. *Tom E*

Alongside *1972* we held three 'Sex Parties', two in the basement at Shoreditch Town Hall and one at the Almeida. I had begun making queer feminist cabaret performance and these parties offered an opportunity to create space for a club/cabaret night to celebrate queer feminist culture and history.

Highlights: Tom and Ben in their undies in a cupboard giving people improvised songs as gifts; Everyone in seventies fancy dress; Jesse Meadows at the make-up table; Jim and Jess getting on board with Lady Vag [Edythe's alter ego] and having whipped cream and water squirted on their face to 'Sexy Boy'.

These parties were a cross-pollination of the theatre-making I had done and was doing with TWE and the queer club work I was just embarking on. It felt like a really special and generous sharing of both creative processes. *Edythe*

I think it was while *1972: The Future of Sex* was on tour, we were approached by The Bike Shed Theatre and Farms for City Children to make a small family show. Edie and I were the remaining members of the company who weren't in work. So we enlisted the great actor and maker Philippa Hogg to make a show called *The Forever Machine*. It was a totally bonkers musical adventure about a time-travel paradox. We performed it in Exeter and a year or so later at Ovalhouse in London. This show is often forgotten, because although Edie also helped make it, I was the only person in the company in it. Let it be known: it did exist, it was a Wardrobe Ensemble show and it was great. *Tom B*

The Forever Machine was maybe my favourite TWE show to produce. We didn't have a set designer so we basically ordered the whole set from Amazon (morally unsound). We ordered loads of fake plants, but when they arrived they were tiny so we had to go on an emergency mission round Exeter looking for fake trees. *Hannah*

It was financially tricky and our parents said classic things like 'When are you going to get a proper job?' or just 'Oh dear.' We made more shows! We got published – eek! We ran loads of workshops. We made the move from small scale to mid-scale, which may sound like theatre jargon, but it meant we could make bigger shows and play to more people. *Emily*

Education, Education, Education

We're back in the room. Twelve of us. The whole gang. After making a few projects with smaller numbers from the ensemble it's exciting to have so many minds and bodies and storytellers in the room again. *Helena*

I remember arriving at day one of R&D thinking, 'What do I have to bring to this room? I've been fucking around in Berlin for a year.' My character would go on to be Tobias, a German teaching assistant, who was based on my roommate in Berlin and whose viewpoint consisted of a mishmash of things I noticed during my year in Germany. I start to understand what people mean when they talk about 'life experience', and I start to appreciate how valuable the company is as a 'life-experience processor'. *James*

We did our first work-in-progress sharing of *Education, Education, Education* on the main stage at Bristol Old Vic as part of Ferment Fortnight. It was all part of the plan for scaling up, but the night before I thought what on earth have I done, we can't send them out there. Luckily it went amazingly, although Edie chipped a huge chunk of paint out of the wall with a chair, which is still there. *Hannah*

Hours of discussion in the pub after rehearsals, talking about patriotism, politics, Britain, colonialism, national pride, and how these things manifested in our rehearsal room and our own relationships. It was the first time I'd properly thought about these things. *James*

Royal & Derngate Northampton came on as co-producers. They put a huge amount of trust in us and we will always be so grateful to them. We had to find another co-producer and also commit to fundraising some money ourselves. We asked Shoreditch Town Hall again and unbelievably they said 'Yes'. *Hannah*

We're invited to perform a couple of one-offs of *1972* at the Almeida over *Education* rehearsals. Anne and I break up the night before our first show. I give one of the best performances of my life. *James*

We met the sound designer Ben Grant in a pub one evening after rehearsals for another show. We'd been given his name by another sound designer who couldn't work on the show as he was too busy. He seemed nice so we asked him to come on board. We subsequently found out he was a total genius and have worked with him ever since. We also found out he had a Number 1 hit in the UK dance charts under the name of Pedro 123. *Hannah*

Making *Education* was massive for the company and one of the things I am most proud of, both as a show but also in terms of a step-change for the company. Away from the making of the show, Hannah and I spent a lot of time worrying about money and logistics. We sat on a train coming back from Northampton after a model-box sharing with a £40,000+ hole in the budget, I was panicking a little, and Hannah (although I'm sure panicking inside) remained calm and calmed me down. She, as ever, found the money... *Jesse J*

We take *Education* to Edinburgh. I plough through the month in a manic, post-break-up energy. We win a Stage Award and a Fringe First. *James*

We've taken a show to Edinburgh every other year for the last nine years. We were also lucky enough to be invited to a small festival in America for two summers in between. Another sunny summer of touring festivals, and a simply magical one at the National means we've spent every single summer together since we formed. I've shared a bed with Helena Middleton more often than my boyfriend. We have unwritten queue rules for a 10:1 person-to-bathroom ratio, and once even made a bath mat with our show's carpet offcuts. I've been in the shower whilst someone else is brushing their teeth and another is on the loo. When you spend that much time with people, you go beyond friends, beyond family – you are functioning as one. We love each other dearly and we drive each other mad. We see each other's best and worst. The boundaries of professional and personal get very blurred. We have no leader or boss, we make all decisions as a group of ten, sometimes the sense of yourself as an individual gets completely lost. It's like some weird idealist collective. It's great and it's really tough. *Jesse M*

I think it's important to say that building methods of collectively working and cohabiting together takes real commitment and care. Despite our differences, our individual needs and quirks, everyone wholeheartedly supports each other and is committed to horizontal collective creative practices.

Fostering understanding, holding ourselves and each other accountable for our actions, having difficult conversations and resolving conflict all take emotional work and we built processes and systems into the company to try and support that. Care and emotional processing is part of the success of a large collective company and that emotional work is ongoing and can always be further improved. I think looking back to see how far we have come in terms of the way we conduct ourselves and relate to each other in a rehearsal room is really special. There is a real commitment to horizontal theatre-making; community building takes work, dedication and investment, and those efforts shouldn't be forgotten. *Edythe*

Around this time, everything was quite overwhelming. You start out producing plays and suddenly you're running a small business that isn't even actually that small any more and you have no idea how to do that. We were learning loads and working more than ever, but we didn't really have any money to sustain ourselves in between shows. I taught a producing module at London Metropolitan University which felt like being successful, but I'd leave lectures and go start a shift in a restaurant. I decided not to tell my students that's what I was doing so I'd look like a proper professional, but in hindsight I wish I'd been more honest. *Hannah*

We tour *Education*. We sell out our run of the Bristol Old Vic main stage. On our opening night, the playtexts arrive – the first time we've been published. BOV also unveil a blue plaque in the new rehearsal room, which is where the old Wardrobe used to be:

Made in Bristol

The Wardrobe Ensemble

Born here

2011

It's a lot for one day. *James*

Many things have changed over the course of our touring lives. We've gone from washing costumes only once through an entire month of Ed Fringe to having a dedicated daily laundry rota to keep us fresh. We've been lucky enough to go from only just covering our own expenses to being paid a weekly fee for our work. We now have an entourage, a wonderful extended family of creatives who mastermind our get-ins and techs and generally make our lives infinitely easier and better. Some touring things have certainly not changed. How many hours we spend on trains, or rather running for trains, I think will never change. Our pre-show warm-ups continue to get sillier and weirder and now draw audiences in the form of ushers and theatre staff. I dread to think what they make of us. We are only really serious when discussing food – our whole day is centred around it. *Kerry*

Some of us spend a tough, snowy Christmas performing *Wind in the Willows* in Corby. I miss my first-ever Christmas at home and spend it with Tom and Em instead. Hannah and I get into a relationship. I don't tell Kerry and that really upsets her. *James*

Wind in the Willows was a hard show for a number of different reasons, but when all is said and done, one that I am very proud of. However, the process was painful at times. It is one of the only times I have ever felt like the company was close to mutiny. I was changing the ending under pressure from the co-producers and the company did not like it – they elected Jimmy to be the spokesperson and he left the stage to come and have a word with me. What they did not realise was that due to them being on radio mics I had already heard the whole conversation. I told Jimmy to get back onstage and we carried on, I really wanted to cry. After press night when Hannah, Ben Grant, Kate Bunce (our designer) and I got on the train back to London with four bottles of prosecco, it's fair to say we (I) got more than a little drunk. *Jesse J*

South Western

In the summer of 2018 we made a show very close to our hearts. *South Western*. In many ways it was a bit of an ode to the South West. A Spaghetti Western set in our motherland. We did our initial R&D at Meadows' mum and dad's house in Lostwithiel, down in Cornwall. We thought rehearsing in the region might inform the show. I think it did. Regardless, we had a lovely time. We all stayed together, cooked together, worked together. We had barbecues by the stream and hashed out a script before heading back to Bristol for more rehearsals in Victoria Road Baptist Church. Or, in the words of Tom Brennan, Vicky P Bappy C. *Tom E*

I decide to sit out *South Western*. I feel burnt out and need a rest. I'm in London for two solid months. I get into a routine, I do activities, I see my friends regularly. I get a summer to myself. I realise I haven't done this in seven years. *James N*

Looking back at the making of the show, I have such fond memories. It was a steaming hot summer. The World Cup was on. England got to the semi final. We had a gay old time. *Tom E*

I get quite invested in these damn shows. *South Western* was difficult, because it was big and ambitious, and yet we had a very short development process in comparison to *1972* or *Education*. It was my birthday halfway through rehearsals and Emily took me out for breakfast before we started the day's work. I sat in a coffee shop and just burst into tears and wept and wept. I had a proper little breakdown. I kept saying, 'Can we just stop for a bit?' I didn't want to disappoint anyone in the company and the pressure for the show to be a success felt so overwhelming. It's so easy to forget that it's just a show. *Tom B*

South Western was my first return to acting in over five years. I was petrified. I had a great time, but I was very nervous for most of the time apart from the last performance. I would like to say that the reason was because I had relaxed into it and become more comfortable. The reality is that I had just found out that Rachel was pregnant and the overriding emotion had changed from nervousness to PANIC. That show is all a bit of a blur. *Jesse J*

There was a day during the *South Western* run when we were all in the dressing rooms preparing for a matinee and Jesse Jones came in and told us there was something he had to tell us. Rachel is pregnant. Silence. Nobody moved. I think I even laughed. Surely this was a 'Jesse Jones inappropriate joke' special. Then I looked at him. He was hugging a pillar and all the colour had drained from his face. He was serious. The penny dropped. We all moved to him and hugged him, our jaws on the floor. Frank turned one a few months ago. The first Wardrobe baby. We adore you. *Kerry*

The Star Seekers II

The Star Seekers at the National. Summer 2018. We arrive giddy, on cloud nine, absolutely the most enthusiastic people in the theatre. We go to the backstage bar in the evenings and act VERY uncool when we see famous people: Imelda Staunton, Simon Russell Beale, Alison Steadman, Ciaran Hinds.

During the tech, the lighting designer, Michael, tells me that there is a bit of money left in the budget, he asks whether I want to buy back-up batteries. I reply, 'That doesn't sound very fun, what else can I have?' He jokingly mentions a glitter drop and before I know it the production manager, Sarah, is calling me over asking me exactly what I would like. I want big pieces of glitter to fall from the ceiling at the end of the show. I get my glitter. The kids go mad and dance in it as it falls, trying to catch it, then gathering it up from the floor.

Throughout tech, dress and first shows I have a terrible tummy, a mixture of nerves and something I ate in Greece the week previously, or so I think. Two weeks later, the diarrhoea has turned to cramps and extreme nausea. I am a frequent user of the disabled loo which is opposite Ralph Fiennes' dressing room as he rehearses for *Antony and Cleopatra*. One day I exit the toilet as he exits his room. We catch eyes and I RUN AWAY. I then proceed to tell everyone about my encounter, 'The English Patient! The English Patient!' Tummy gets worse and on my day off I get soaked as I drag myself to a walk-in centre.

The result of which is three empty vials for me to fill and to hand into the Department of Tropical Diseases. It somehow feels appropriate that whilst I'm living out my absolute dream job I should also be desperately trying to poop into a tiny pot.

There is a lot of buzz around the building about the show, I get the feeling the staff are happy to see a show which is so unashamedly silly. A show made by a group of friends from Bristol who are just over the moon to be there. *Helena*

Education, Education, Education II

I remember the first time we thought the show might transfer to the West End, Hannah and I were walking over Waterloo Bridge after a meeting at the Trafalgar Entertainment office on the Strand. The possibility was very scary and very exciting. *Jesse J*

Education, Education, Education transfers to Trafalgar Studios. The West End. It's a surreal experience and it spooks a lot of us. The marketing: *Friends*-style photoshoots in Trafalgar Square; posters on the Tube; a van with the show info driving around central London, blaring out 'Things Can Only Get Better'. *James*

When *Education* is confirmed for Trafalgar Studios I already have flights booked for Japan. I get back the day before press night. I watch the show dazed and confused, clutching a tiny Ty beanie baby and a bottle of champagne. We go to a party across the road. We all meet Paul Chuckle. *Helena*

We found out that we got a pretty game-changing amount of Arts Council funding the day that *Education* opened. It meant I could leave the restaurant and work for the company full-time. I was in the basement of Trafalgar Studios sewing buttons onto a King Arthur costume (incredibly badly – it all had to be redone by somebody who can actually sew). *Hannah*

Performing the show at Trafalgar Studios felt like the culmination of many years of graft and so it was difficult to keep our feet on the ground and our heads from floating away in the lead-up to the opening week. It was quite overwhelming at first. What with the photoshoots, the marketing, the impending 'press night', the hope of this being our 'big break'. It all felt very different to anything we had done before. Not least because we all had our own dressing room which, in a company of upwards of ten people, is unheard of. But once the opening show had been performed, the press night passed, the cobwebs dusted away, the nerves settled, and the reviews accumulated (and they were overwhelmingly average), it became apparent that performing on a stage in London to a group of people need not be any different from performing on a stage in, say, Hull or Corby to a group of people. *Tom E*

We don't sell well. We lose some people a lot of money. *James*

I was unable to open *Education, Education, Education* in the West End because I had to have some pretty major surgery for endometriosis. I'll be honest: it broke me. Feeling so tremendously proud of what we'd managed to achieve, but not actually being there to experience it with everyone was very difficult. Luckily I was well enough to join for the final weeks of the run. In hindsight, my body probably wasn't ready, but there was no way I was going to willingly pass up that opportunity. Turns out, performing on the West End is very similar to performing anywhere else. Who knew? *Kerry*

Before one of our final shows, as we had one of our daily huddles backstage before 'beginners' were called, Jesse Meadows reminded us to take a deep breath after the show had finished, just before the lights came back up for the bow. She encouraged us to take it in, acknowledge who we were standing alongside, and remember to remember that moment. I will. *Tom E*

The Last of the Pelican Daughters

And finally, *The Pelican Daughters*. The first time I've properly thought about family, inheritance, class, growing up, changing and staying the same, how I relate to my family, my friends, The Wardrobe Ensemble. What it means not to be a child any more. To shoulder financial and emotional responsibility. To face losing the ones close to you. *James*

The title comes from a *King Lear* line that both me and my sister had to memorise for our GCSE English exams. My mum picked up on it and used to shout 'Pelican daughters' at us when we were being annoying or wanting things. When we decided to use it as a title I told my mum that we'd named the play after her, but she had no memory of the phrase at all. *Hannah*

It's a long, hard process. It's our most personal yet and our most complex yet. We write like we've never written before, and act like we've never acted before. It's scary to make and scary to perform because it's close to the bone. Very, very personal. I'm very proud of it and I'm quite intimidated by it. *James*

On week three of making *Pelican Daughters*, Frank got ill for the first time in his life. We were rehearsing in Northampton, and Rachel and Frank were in Bristol, and I felt awful for not being there. Tom told me to get on a train and everyone gave me a hug and sent me on my way. I felt held and loved in a way that made me so grateful and privileged to be part of this company. *Jesse J*

One day, during our run at Trafalgar Studios, I met with a directing student to give her advice about the industry that I work in, but still have no idea about. During the course of this chat we start to talk about *Pelican Daughters* and as I'm talking I have a realisation: This show is us. This family, the Pelicans are us, The Wardrobe Ensemble. The relationships, the love, the silliness, the frustrations, the exasperation, the sheer complexity, is all us. A heightened, unhinged, ridiculous version of us, but still us. *James*

We went to Edinburgh. I ordered square flyers without checking the actual dimensions of the square I was ordering. I figured a square is a square. They arrived and they were HUGE. We pretended it's what we meant all along. *Hannah*

Performing at the Fringe this time was much harder than we anticipated. Every element of this production is more ambitious than previously. The set is huge. It doesn't fit in the performance space, so we have to saw it in half and attach hinges. The air-con is so loud that there is a constant buzz in the background of the show that I can never quite block out, and I don't think the audience can either. We are split between two houses for the first time. I have my own room and even an en-suite for the first time (unheard of!), but I find myself lonely and missing the chaotic communal vibes. It takes longer than usual to get into the groove of the show, but it is always a blessing to have a whole month of performing to hone a production. *Jesse M*

In September 2019 (after nine years – such a long time!) I left TWE. I left to focus on my visual art and performance practice. I'd been living in New York for a few years and I'd moved away from narrative theatre-making towards material and somatic movement practices. Invested in the queer, dyke and trans spaces that I had come to call home, my work shifted in focus, advocating for and working from within my queer communities. TWE gave space for me to grow, to discover my queerness with love and encouragement, and to build my art practice with their full support. *Edythe*

Last week, we went to the ten-year anniversary of the Made in Bristol programme and performed *RIOT* in all its 2011 originality. We felt proud of what our younger selves had made, but also realised how much we've developed. *The Last of the Pelican Daughters* is a family drama. It's an epic, emotional one. We've made it in a different way, perhaps a more traditional way. We gravitated towards writing tasks rather than physical ones. The show has full 3D characters that don't represent a specific concept. There are lots of themes rather than one. Perhaps it's a show that leans more to the theatrical 'status quo', but for a devising company that writes collaboratively, it feels pretty cool. It's not to say that we won't make shows like *RIOT*, where we throw each other around, but it feels exciting that we're in a position to challenge ourselves creatively. We might make a comedy next. *Emily*

Re-rehearsing *Pelican* for tour was a total joy. Having an opportunity to interrogate the play with some fresh voices gives us a chance to fall in love with it again. The new cast are fantastic and very quickly become part of the fold. During our rehearsals, the coronavirus conversation starts to heat up. We were meant to be taking a show to Indonesia in May and that gets cancelled. During our first week of tour we are in Northampton and there is a lot of corona talk, some of us are more anxious than others. We get through a lot of anti-bac. I am genuinely unwell the whole week and I can't tell if people are joking or not about their concern. We have a week off tour and instead do a new R&D together in London. Every day there is a greater underlying sense of unease. We all feel icky taking the Tube. Posters go up in the building about hand-washing procedures. Sally comes in with a temperature and we send her home. If anyone feels slightly unwell it creates a flurry of panic. We all constantly check our news apps. The tour isn't selling very well as people are clearly staying away from public spaces.

On the Thursday we end rehearsals early and have a 'briefing' where Hannah talks through every possibility and our action plan; if Sally stays ill, if one of the cast has to isolate, if theatres close... We bank on having at least one more week (at the Nuffield in Southampton) before anything is officially decided. Sally gets better. We go to Frank's first birthday party. Kerry and Tom drive to Southampton. The set gets put up on the Monday and I pack along with the rest of the cast, ready to arrive the next day. On Monday night at 5.30 p.m. Boris Johnson announces that people should avoid going to theatres, but puts it onto the theatres to decide whether to close. At 6 p.m. we have a company meeting where it quickly becomes apparent that even if the Nuffield stays open, it would be irresponsible to carry on with the tour. I am Skyping everyone on my phone, standing looking out to the sea in Clevedon, and in an instant our future dissolves into it. I cannot comprehend what is happening. We are all heartbroken but everything is suddenly out of our control and there are much bigger things happening in the world. The next morning every theatre in the country announces closure for the foreseeable future. It is a sad, dark, scary time for an industry that relies on the gathering of crowds. Everything is now an unknown. I'm currently writing this on the first day of lockdown in Britain and we have been sent the proofs from Nick Hern Books. We're very grateful that they will still be publishing our script. I'm very grateful we spent that week together in London. *Jesse M*

We were in the middle of the get-in when the advice to shut theatres as a result of COVID-19 happened. We never got to perform the show there, the Nuffield has gone into administration and we cancelled the tour. In lockdown we have been Zooming a few times a week as a company and it's a weird and hard time, but we have each other and we are very lucky that that is the case. I think it might be time to get that coat-hanger tattoo. *Jesse J*

I suppose trying to articulate what has gone on between us all these past nine years is impossible. There's an attempt to be honest and personal in this history. But we all know that there are details in our story (both positive and negative) that are far too personal to acknowledge here. It feels important to say: it was a better time than can be expressed here, but also a substantially worse one. As I read this over, it doesn't do any kind of justice to the ever-shifting tensions, sleepless nights, sweating, shivers, tears and laughter, all-out fights and subtle frustrations, the depth of the conversations and stupidity of the in-jokes. *Tom B*

Production Notes

The Last of the Pelican Daughters is a 'family drama' that (both ironically and with total heartfelt conviction) sits within the tradition of the family dramas of the past. We were inspired by a wide range of forms, styles and playwrights: Aeschylus and Euripides, Shakespeare, Chekhov, Ibsen, Lillian Hellman, Edward Albee, Alan Ayckbourn and Wes Anderson, among many others. It didn't go unnoticed that the majority of our influences were white men. We reimagined the tradition in our own image and we encourage any future productions to do the same.

Although the dialogue is often naturalistic, the playing style and blocking needn't be. The effect of which is to balance the grand, timeless and traditional with the particular contemporary dilemmas and dynamics of the Pelican family.

Stage directions, music and design choices refer to our original production, but future incarnations should feel free to deviate.

We used projection to title each 'chapter' and to add visual context. This information might be given to the audience in a host of other ways.

The house should feel like another living, breathing character.

In our production, we began in a large empty pink room with a front door upstage-centre. Over the course of the production, we introduced any set and props that we needed. Eventually in the final scene the space resembled a fairly naturalistic lived-in dining room, with a record player, coat stand, chairs and a big table.

During the dance sequence at the end of Chapter Six, a secret room was revealed within our set. This space was Mum's room, untouched and preserved since she left it the year before. At various moments throughout the production, the walls revealed cracks or veins that led to Mum's room.

The house was pink. Mum's dress, her room and everything within it was a deep red.

In our production, the sisters take it in turns to play Mum in their memories. This needn't be the case.

Granny was played by a skeleton in a wheelchair and voiced by the actor who plays Lara and Solicitor using a microphone. The same actor enters in period dress to play Young Granny.

The price of the house, and thus the children's inheritance, were based on the national average. Feel free to change.

The Last of the Pelican Daughters was first performed at The Pleasance Courtyard as part of the 2019 Edinburgh Festival Fringe, with the following cast:

DERREN	Tom England
GRANNY/LARA/SOLICITOR	Emily Greenslade
MAYA	Sara Lessore
JOY	Kerry Lovell
STORM	Jesse Meadows
SAGE	Helena Middleton
LUKE	James Newton
DODO	Ben Vardy

The production toured in 2020, opening at Royal & Derngate Northampton, with the following cast changes:

MAYA	Sally Cheng
DODO	Laurie Jamieson
SAGE	Beatrice Scirocchi

The tour was cancelled on 17 March 2020 due to COVID-19.

A Wardrobe Ensemble, Complicité and Royal & Derngate Northampton co-production in association with Bristol Old Vic and The Pleasance.

Written and devised by Tom Brennan, Tom England, Emily Greenslade, Jesse Jones, Sara Lessore, Kerry Lovell, Jesse Meadows, Helena Middleton, James Newton and Ben Vardy.

Co-directors	Tom Brennan and Jesse Jones
Designer	Ruby Spencer Pugh
Sound Designer	Benjamin Grant
Lighting Designer	Jessica Hung Han Yun
Wardrobe Supervisor	Hannah Marshall
Associate Sound Designer	Joe Dines
Assistant Director	Georgia Tillery
Dramaturg	Bea Roberts

Production Manager	The Production Family
Technical Stage Manager	Fergus Waldron
Stage Manager	Maddy Wade
Assistant Stage Manager	Will Edwards
Sound Engineer	Tom Crosley-Thorne
Show Image	James Bullimore
Poster Design	Will Brady
Production Photography	Graeme Braidwood
Producer for The Wardrobe Ensemble	Hannah Smith

Additional material by Oliver Alvin-Wilson, Sally Cheng, Kayode Ewumi, Paul Hunter, Laurie Jamieson, Shaheen Khan, Beatrice Scirocchi, Temi Wilkey and Edythe Woolley.

THE LAST OF THE PELICAN DAUGHTERS

The Wardrobe Ensemble

Characters

JOY PELICAN, *the eldest child of Rosemary Pelican*
DERREN, *her husband, from Swindon*
STORM PELICAN, *the second-born child of Rosemary Pelican*
SAGE PELICAN, *the third-born child of Rosemary Pelican,*
    an artist
MAYA PELICAN, *the youngest daughter of Rosemary Pelican*
DODO, *her life partner, American*
GRANNY, *old*
LARA, *her carer*
SOLICITOR, *Susie Stephens of Stephen Stephens and Sons*
    Solicitors
LUKE, *a difficult brother, the youngest child of Rosemary*
    Pelican

… at the end of a speech means it trails off or it indicates a pressure, expectation or desire to speak.

/ means an interruption when the next character's text should start.

Prologue – Origin Stories

Projection: 'The Last of the Pelican Daughters'.

Dimly lit room. Orchestral strings start tuning up.

Projection: '"They fuck you up, your mum and dad.
They may not mean to, but they do.
They fill you with the faults they had.
And add some extra just for you." – Philip Larkin'

Projection: '"Hold dear to your parents for it is a scary and confusing world without them." – Emily Dickinson'

Projection: '"Remember who you are." – Mufasa'

The four DAUGHTERS enter after the Mufasa quote fades, wearing the same red dress.

JOY. Imagine an end-terrace Victorian house.

MAYA. On Mina Road.

STORM. In St Werburghs.

SAGE. In Bristol. Three bedrooms.

JOY. A living room.

MAYA. An upstairs bathroom and a downstairs toilet.

STORM. An open-plan kitchen diner and a nice-size garden.

JOY. Imagine a large dining table.

SAGE. Pink walls.

JOY. Very pink walls.

MAYA. Exposed floorboards.

STORM. Frida Kahlo painted on the chimney breast.

MAYA. Statuettes of Shiva and Buddha and Sau Sing Gong.

SAGE. Bookshelves filled with de Beauvoir and Butler and Plath.

JOY. This is where my daughters –

MAYA. The Pelican daughters –

JOY. Learned their values.

MAYA. Where I taught them to look at the world and imagine.

SAGE. Imagine a whole different way of being.

STORM. In 1977 this house was valued at...

Projection: '£6,067'.

JOY. A pint of milk cost...

Projection: '£0.12'.

SAGE. The Prime Minister was...

Projection: Photo of James Callaghan.

MAYA. And the Queen looked like...

Projection: Photo of the cover of the 'God Save the Queen' single by Sex Pistols.

STORM. And it was in that year that I bought this house using my student grant as a deposit.

JOY. This is where my children grew up.

SAGE. Where they had their first periods.

STORM. Where they fought each other.

JOY. It's where they were born.

Music. 'Damaged Goods' by Gang of Four. As each sister tells her birth story, she takes off her red dress.

Projection: 'Joy 1984'.

Joy, meaning delight or great pleasure, was born in September 1984. The agony of the thirty-six-hour labour was endured with only paracetamol and gas and air. A handy trainee midwife with a set of forceps, clamped down on my skull and yanked, ripping my mother's vagina wider than the Avon Gorge. It was a day of pure joy. Joy.

Projection: 'Storm 1987'.

STORM. Storm. A disturbance of the normal condition of the atmosphere. I was born during the hurricane-strength winds of 1987 on the night of the most destructive weather event in almost three hundred years. As Michael Fish cried himself to sleep, I tore through my mum's perineum. Tiles fell out of the sky, trees toppled, the country came to a halt, and I gushed into the world at a hundred and fifteen miles per hour onto the kitchen table. My mother collapsed. My sister screamed from her cot upstairs. Storm.

Projection: 'Sage 1990'.

SAGE. Sage, from the Latin *sapere*, meaning to taste, to discern, to be wise. In November 1990, as my mum push, push, pushed me out into a paddling pool in the living room, Thatcher was pushed out of Downing Street. Good job, Mum. Sage.

Projection: 'Maya 1995'.

MAYA. Maya, Latin for great, was born in 1995. My mum sneezed and out I skipped, three weeks early, cutting short a family holiday to the Norfolk Broads. My mum would joke at every family gathering for the next twenty years that it was the only time I ever arrived early. Maya.

The SISTERS *are in their mum's house.*

SAGE. Imagine this is where I drew my first picture.

MAYA. Where there are notches on the door that track our heights.

JOY. A strange smell that never quite goes away.

STORM. Mum's endless attempts at vegetarian cooking.

SAGE. Mum was many things but she was not a cook.

STORM. This house was a meeting place for Mum's friends.

SAGE. Coming and going, staying the night. Big parties.

JOY. Weirdos.

SAGE. Making placards in the kitchen.

STORM. 'Bollocks to the bypass.'

MAYA. 'Bulldozer fascists.'

STORM. Packing for festivals.

JOY. Festival after festival after festival.

MAYA. Mum's music.

SAGE. The best record collection. Minnie Riperton, Patti Smith.

JOY. Always music in the house.

STORM. Mum's taste knew no bounds.

SAGE. We'd make up dances to Grace Jones.

JOY. And Mum. At the centre of it all.

MAYA. Our mum, Rosemary Pelican, who lived in this house for forty-one years. Forty-one years before...

'Symphony No. 45 in F-Sharp Minor "Farewell": IV. Finale: Presto – Adagio' by Franz Joseph Haydn plays. They exit. SOLICITOR *enters*.

SOLICITOR. Hi, this is Susie Stephens of Stephen Stephens and Sons Solicitors. I'm your solicitor. We spoke on Monday. If you could give me a call back, that'd be great. It's regarding your dead mum's will, deceased mum's will, mum's will. Haha. God. Sorry. Call me back. Okay, thanks. Bye bye. Bye. Bye.

SOLICITOR *exits*.

Chapter One – Flying Home

STORM *is standing alone in the house, holding her mum's red dress.* SAGE *enters.*

SAGE. Hello, house!

(*Referring to dress.*) That's Mum's.

STORM. Yeah.

SAGE. Playing dress up?

STORM. Just sorting.

STORM *goes to hug her.*

SAGE. Don't touch me, I'm gross. The air con on the Megabus was broken. Again.

STORM. What's in the bag?

SAGE. I've got all the cake stuff. Cost me a fortune. How many candles do you think is too many?

STORM. Err…

SAGE. And I bought three packs of hundreds and thousands!

STORM. Great.

SAGE. Where am I sleeping?

STORM. You're sharing with Maya.

SAGE. Alright. She here yet?

STORM. Obviously not. She's bringing a boyfriend.

SAGE. Oh god. The one she met in Bali?

STORM. I don't know. I've lost track. He's got a weird name.

SAGE. Well, if we're sharing I'm going to need a strict no-sex rule.

STORM. Gross, they're not gonna do that in the bunk beds.

SAGE. Never stopped me! I need a shower.

SAGE *starts to leave.*

STORM. Can I just –

SAGE. Before you ask, Dora's not coming, we're on a break.

STORM. Right.

SAGE. Fuck her.

SAGE *exits*.

STORM *looks at the dress again.* JOY *enters with a bag for life.*

JOY. Hello, house.

(*Referring to dress.*) That's Mum's.

STORM. Joy!

STORM *hugs* JOY *who has her hands full.* DERREN *enters with more bags.*

DERREN. Hey, Storm! I dunno that we've got enough here.

JOY. We need to get it in the fridge.

STORM. What did you get?

JOY. A ham, some dips, a couple of bottles of white.

STORM. A ham?

DERREN *goes to the kitchen with shopping bags.*

JOY. Just a couple of bits and bobs.

STORM. Ah, okay, I can chip in…

JOY. Don't worry about it.

STORM. Are you sure?

JOY. Yeah of course.

DERREN *re-enters.*

STORM. Derren, thank you so much!

DERREN. Oh no, don't worry about it.

JOY. Right, are we sleeping in Mum's room?

STORM. Actually I've put you in mine.

JOY. Where are you gonna sleep?

STORM. I'll stay down here, with Granny.

JOY. Storm, that doesn't make any sense, you might as well
    have your own room and then /

STORM. I just thought... it's just... if you want to you can...
    I'd just rather...

DERREN. I'll just get the rest of the booze from the car. We
    bought a shit-ton of shitty prosecco. I forgot how pink this
    house is!

    DERREN *goes back out the front door.*

STORM. I'm sorry.

JOY. It's fine.

    SAGE *enters.*

SAGE. Stormy, where have you put the towels? (*Sees* JOY.)
    Alright, mate! Big night tonight!

JOY. Look at your hair!

SAGE. I grew it out. Do you like it?

JOY. Yeah I do.

    DERREN *enters carrying more bags.*

DERREN. Hey, Sage.

SAGE. Swindon's here! Yes!

    She chases him out.

JOY. When does Granny get here?

STORM. Five-ish.

    JOY *leaves. A moment of* STORM *alone.*

    MAYA *and* DODO *enter.*

MAYA. / They're gonna love you. I can't wait for you to meet
    them. We're gonna have the best time.

DODO. / I love it, I love it so much, it's beautiful, I love you,
    I love you – (*Etc.*)

MAYA *and* DODO *kiss*.

STORM. Hello!

MAYA. Oh my god! Stormy! I've missed you so much.

   MAYA *and* STORM *hug*.

STORM. You look different.

MAYA. No I don't. Is Luke here yet?

STORM. He's not coming.

MAYA. Oh. Where are we sleeping?

STORM. You're with Sage in your old room.

MAYA. I thought we could sleep in Mum's.

STORM. I've made the beds now so.

MAYA. Boyfriend, sister, sister, boyfriend. Now I must go and powder my nose aka take a massive dump. Hellooo, house!

   MAYA *leaves*.

DODO. Hi, my name's Dodo. Like the bird.

STORM. Storm. Like the weather.

DODO. Cool name, Storm.

   DODO *leaves*. STORM *looks down at the dress and screams into it. 'Symphony No. 45 in F-Sharp Minor "Farewell": IV. Finale: Presto – Adagio' by Franz Joseph Haydn plays*.

Chapter Two – Together

Everyone gathers for story-sharing.

JOY. And the train man told us we had to walk all the way to the other station.

STORM. To Exeter St Davids.

JOY. Which is like a million miles away.

DERREN. Not quite a million miles, Joy.

JOY. Well, far enough. And this guy in this suit –

SAGE. Floppy hair, public school, you know the type –

JOY. He's like 'Oh please! Let me help you with that.'
I remember Mum was holding my hand.

SAGE. And Mum said, 'I don't need any help, thanks.'

JOY. Then he said, 'It's quite a long way, and that's quite a big
suitcase.'

MAYA. Lol.

DODO. No way.

SAGE. And she turns around and says, 'I know how far it is and
I know how heavy my suitcase is, thank you.'

JOY. And then he says, 'I cannot let a beautiful woman like you
carry that huge suitcase all the way to St Davids.' And then
she just watched him as he picked up the bag and heaves it
away from us.

STORM. And we stood there looking back and forth between
Mum and this guy getting smaller and smaller.

JOY. And then she ran. Sprinted.

SAGE. So fast.

JOY. And then she just picked him up!

DODO. What?

   SAGE *picks up* STORM.

MAYA. Lifted him right up. Up in the air like this.

   She lifts her arms. SAGE *drops* STORM.

JOY. And then he said, 'Put me down, you bloody maniac.'

SAGE/JOY. 'You. Bloody. Maniac.'

SAGE. And then she carried him all the way to the other
station.

MAYA. With the suitcase.

JOY. Bullshit. She lifted him up for about two seconds.

SAGE. No.

JOY. He dropped the suitcase straight away.

MAYA. No, Joy, she carried him all the way to the station. I remember. And then put him down.

JOY. You don't remember. You were a baby.

MAYA. I was five.

STORM. You weren't five.

JOY. You were one and I was twelve. And I remember because that was the year I kissed Andy Vowles.

MAYA/SAGE/STORM. Errrgghh, Vowlesy!

JOY. He was cute.

MAYA. Joy, I was five.

JOY. Whatever. Happy birthday Mum!

ALL. Happy birthday Mum.

MAYA. I was five.

DODO. You *were* five. Of course you were five.

STORM. Can I just say, there's something I wanted to –

SAGE. Hey! Do you remember the cake story?

STORM. Sage, if I could just have a moment –

JOY. The cake story?

SAGE. Yeah.

MAYA. On Mum's birthday!

JOY. Oh yeah!

DERREN. Ooh, I haven't heard this one.

SAGE. So, it was a tradition that at the stroke of midnight on Mum's birthday we would sit on her bed and eat a huge cake.

DERREN. Oh crumbs!

MAYA. Haha.

SAGE. Which we will all be doing tonight. Acknowledgement?

ALL. Acknowledgement!

SAGE. Cake is in the oven. Mum's original recipe.

DERREN. Looking forward to that!

SAGE. So, it was Mum's birthday and she had been working loads and for the first time ever she'd forgotten to make the cake.

MAYA. Major sin.

JOY. Unheard of.

SAGE. I was gutted.

STORM. She wouldn't stop crying.

JOY. She loves cake.

DERREN. Who doesn't?

SAGE. I was ten! Anyway, so Mum herded all of us into the Volvo.

MAYA. Me and Storm always sat in the boot seats and pulled faces at the drivers.

DODO. That is so adorable.

SAGE. We pulled up to the big Tesco in Eastville, and she turns to us and says, very calmly: 'I want you to remember that corporations are not people. This is a victimless crime. All for one – '

JOY/MAYA/SAGE. 'And one for all!'

MAYA. And we run into Tesco's!

JOY. GO!

JOY/MAYA. Pelicans! Pelicans! Pelicans!

JOY. Maya causes a distraction.

MAYA. I pour icing sugar all over my head.

SAGE. And we grab whatever we want.

JOY. We stuff our pockets full of cupcakes and gingerbread men.

STORM. It was really stressful.

DERREN. Hang on, you stole them?

MAYA. It's only Tesco's!

SAGE. Eat the change you want to see, Derren!

DODO. Preach, sister!

JOY. I can't believe we did that.

MAYA. Oh shut up you loved it.

DERREN. Joy?

SAGE. And Mum sneaks out the BIGGEST birthday cake in the shop under her coat.

MAYA. And just as we leave, this security guard says, 'What have you got under there?' and she says, 'I'm pregnant!'

SAGE. And that night we got onto her bed and ate and ate and ate.

JOY. And then we all fell asleep on her bed.

SAGE. And we woke up two hours later and we all threw up. Best birthday ever. Mum was so cool.

STORM. I've got something /

DERREN. I've got one.

General noises of encouragement: 'Go on, Derren!', 'Woo, Derren!', 'Derren steps up to the plate', etc.

DODO. Tell us, Deraine.

DERREN. Derren.

DODO. Darren? Deraine?

MAYA. You'll get there.

DODO. I think I've got it, babe.

DERREN. So it's the first time I'd met these guys' mum and I was terrified.

JOY. He had a panic attack in the car on the way.

DERREN. I didn't… It wasn't a panic attack, I have allergies. Anyway, I arrive, she opens the door and just looks at me with complete disdain. Actually, Joy, you look at me like that sometimes, same look.

SAGE. She does!

JOY. I do do that.

DERREN. So these guys are all in the kitchen catching up, I'm stood in the corner trying to be invisible, right, then suddenly your mum turns to me and says, 'Can you pass the paprika?'

DODO. Yeah?

DERREN. But I can see, she's right next to it. She's literally stood next to the spice rack.

MAYA. Power play.

SAGE. Total power play.

JOY. It's a classic.

DERREN. Exactly! And I know that and that's pissed me right off, so straight away I say, 'Get it yourself.'

ALL. Woooow, oh my god… (*Etc.*)

DERREN. And she stares at me for like, two whole minutes.

JOY. Five seconds.

DERREN. Yeah okay. And eventually she says, 'He can stay.'

ALL. Awwww. Well done, Derren, Derren passed the test… (*Etc.*)

DODO. Would you guys mind if I said a few words? Would that be okay, Maya?

MAYA. That would be lovely, Dodo.

DODO. Thanks, babe. I'd just like to say that although
I obviously never met your guys' mom, I have been feeling
her, like, actual physical presence, right here in this room.
And at first it was kind of freaking me out. But then
I realised that it's all down to you guys. You amazing,
headstrong, beautiful women who carry all that is good and
pure of your mother inside you, everywhere you go.

And you know what? I know your mom intimately, okay?
Through your words and your actions I know your mom. She
inhabits these walls. She *is* this house.

So here's to you, Rosemary. Mom. The world is a brighter
place for your brief moment on it. Cheers.

An awkward cheers. MAYA *looks embarrassed. She goes to
put a record on.*

SAGE. Anyone want more shitty prosecco?

General 'yeah, yes, let me help you'.

STORM. Excuse me... excuse me... Hey. I'd like to say
something.

MAYA *puts on 'Pull up to the Bumper' by Grace Jones.*
JOY, SAGE *and* MAYA *dance to the song. A choreographed
routine they made up when they were children.*

Sorry, guys! If we could just... I know there's a lot to... can
we do this later?

SAGE. Come on, Stormy! Get involved!

Suddenly we are in STORM*'s memory.* MUM *appears in her
red dress, played by* JOY.

MUM. Come on, Storm, get angry! You need to use your
imagination. I want to see you be passionate about
something!

STORM. I am angry.

MUM. I don't see it. I just see you sitting at home all day on
your laptop.

STORM. I'm making my zine.

MUM. Your zine, fantastic. When I was your age I was out on the picket line getting touched up by the miners.

STORM. Mum!

MUM. But I didn't mind because I knew those boys' hearts were in the right place.

STORM. Gross.

MUM. When's the last time you were touched up by a miner?

STORM. That's not the point.

MUM. You lot, you're always sad, always scared. Get. Up. Off. Your. Ass. Pull your tits up and stand up for yourself. One bit of bad news, and you piss your pants… See this? Greenham Common, barbed wire.

STORM. You always bring up Greenham Common.

MUM. See this? 1976, riot police pinned me down and slashed me with a razor.

STORM. That's your caesarean scar.

MUM. Oh, semantics. When are you moving out?

STORM. Monday.

MUM. Good. Well I'm glad to see you back on your feet again. That course wasn't right for you anyway. Fascists.

STORM. Mum!

MUM. Talking of fascists, I've been called back in to see that god-awful doctor. More effing scans!

STORM. Shall I come with you?

The memory fades. Back to the dance.

STORM *walks over to the record player, turns the record off, takes it off the turntable and smashes it over her head.*

I've made a PowerPoint presentation.

'Symphony No. 45 in F-Sharp Minor "Farewell": IV. Finale: Presto – Adagio' by Franz Joseph Haydn plays.

Chapter Three – The Presentation

STORM. Okay, right, check that works, great. Everyone ready?

JOY. Yeah.

STORM. So, we're gathered here today to celebrate Mum.

Projection: 'Rosemary Pelican 1953–2020'.

Mum was an amazing person, she was kind...

Projection: 'kind' (written in funky clip-art).

Generous...

Projection: 'generous' (written in funky clip-art).

Loving...

Projection: 'loving' (written in funky clip-art).

...and she didn't mind being a bit silly sometimes too.

Projection: 'silly' (written in funky clip-art).

And we all loved her very much.

SAGE. This is really weird and lovely, Stormy.

STORM. Thanks. Now, as you all know Mum was never very interested in her finances.

MAYA. You can say that again!

STORM. And she didn't leave the most detailed will in the world, but on page four...

Projection: Image of excerpt from will.

...as I've mentioned before, it says: 'My estate and assets should be divided fairly between my children.' Note the wording here, 'fairly' –

Projection: Image of excerpt from will with 'fairly' underlined.

...not equally.

Now it's taken Joy and I the last eight months to sort out all the paperwork to sell the house but that's all done now, so thanks, Joy, for helping with that.

JOY. No problem.

STORM. And it looks like, after fees, we should be left with about...

Projection: '£250,000'.

...two hundred and fifty thousand, so roughly fifty grand each.

Projection: Graph of how money is divided.

However, given the amount of time I spent caring for Mum, I think it would be fair for us to each shave a little...

Projection: Amended graph of how money is divided.

...off the top of our amounts, to pay me for that time.

Projection: 'Thank you' cute cat image.

Silence.

SAGE. Are you serious?

STORM. What I'm suggesting is that we shave ten thousand pounds –

Projection: '£10,000 x 4 = £40,000'.

...off everyone's total, so that we can pay me a modest salary, fifteen thousand a year...

Projection: '£10,000 x 4 = £40,000 = 2.5 years at £15,000 per year'.

...for two-and-a-half years of looking after Mum. I think that's fair.

MAYA. Huh.

JOY. You're asking us to pay you a salary?

STORM. Okay not a salary, more a gesture of goodwill. Compensation for that time, for that unpaid labour.

MAYA. Okay. Storm, I don't think you can just decide...

SAGE. Why are you doing this now?

MAYA. Shouldn't Luke be here to talk about this?

STORM. I've already spoken to him, he said he's happy with what I'm suggesting and he couldn't be bothered to come.

JOY. Typical.

STORM. And this isn't me deciding, it's a request from your sister. It's why I wanted us all to come together.

SAGE. That's not why! We're here to celebrate Mum's birthday.

STORM. And we are. We are!

SAGE. You're making this about money and paperwork. She hated all of that shit.

MAYA. I thought you got paid?

STORM. Carer's allowance.

MAYA. Yeah.

JOY. It's not a lot.

STORM. Sixty-four pounds a week.

JOY. Just over three grand a year, yes. Look, Storm, I know how much work you did. But if we're talking about finances, you also lived in this house, rent-free.

STORM. I lost two years of my life, Joy. I was going to go... I was going to... I had plans!

JOY. But you made that choice and we supported you, when you said you would do it.

STORM. I understand that this is complicated.

JOY. Yes it is.

STORM. And maybe there's a conversation to be had about precisely how we split the money...

SAGE. Do you mean like, Joy could pay more because she earns more?

JOY. Now hang on.

SAGE. I'm just trying to resolve this so we can get on with celebrating Mum.

JOY. I shouldn't be punished because I work ten times harder than the rest of you.

STORM/SAGE/MAYA. Ten times harder!?!?

General protests from STORM *and* MAYA.

JOY. I don't mean that. But I do work fourteen-hour days and weekends and I have sacrificed a hell of a lot for my salary.

More protests from STORM *and* SAGE.

JOY *cools off.*

Look, Derren and I have plans. I'm sorry but we need that money.

STORM. I changed her nappies, Joy, I changed her fucking nappies. Do you get that?

JOY. Yes. I get that.

STORM. I had to wipe shit off her legs while she called me a cunt.

JOY. I know.

STORM. And you promised you'd make it up to me.

JOY. With a holiday or something.

STORM. Thanks, Joy! Two years' hard labour compensated with a week in the Costa del Sol.

JOY. Might do you some good to fuck a pool boy.

MAYA. Joy.

STORM. Bitch.

MAYA. Storm! I think we can all acknowledge the initial outrage that Storm's suggestion has caused, this isn't an easy thing to hear and probably wasn't an easy thing to say either. Acknowledgement?

ALL. Acknowledgement.

MAYA. And I'm going to say that, in principle, I'm not averse to Storm's request.

STORM. Thank you.

MAYA. Storm, I love you with every fibre of my being. But I can't give you that money.

STORM. What?

SAGE. Ha.

MAYA. I'm broke. I've got nothing.

STORM. You spent the last year travelling, Maya. You skateboarded down flipping volcanoes.

MAYA. Sandboarded.

STORM. You hiked to Machu fucking Picchu.

MAYA. Mum wanted me to travel.

STORM. And I wanted Mum not to die!

JOY/SAGE/STORM. What?

MAYA. Dodo and I need the money.

JOY. Why?

SAGE. I don't want to talk about this any more.

MAYA. We've just got a lot on.

SAGE. You're hijacking my weekend.

JOY. Our weekend.

SAGE. You're hijacking our weekend.

STORM. I'm sorry, Sage, but this was the only chance I'd get to explain.

JOY. To explain that you're a greedy cow?

STORM. Shut up! When you all get the money from the house that is a gift that none of you have done anything to deserve.

Mum's not here any more. She can't tell us how to split everything. We've got to decide for ourselves, but it's got to be fair!

SAGE*'s memory.* MUM *is played by* STORM. MUM *is listening to 'Imagine' by John Lennon.*

MUM. Shh.

Pause.

SAGE. Mum, I just...

MUM. Quiet, Sage. Close your eyes. Listen.

SAGE *hugs* MUM.

SAGE. This is boring.

MUM. Sage! This is not boring, this is the most important song of all time. Now close your eyes and listen, and really listen this time. Imagine no possessions. I wonder if you can... do do do do dododo.

He knew. He knew. John Lennon, you really were the best of us.

Why don't you grow your hair out? I liked it when it was long.

SAGE. What, so I can look like you?

MUM. You'd be lucky. Do you need any money?

SAGE. I'm fine.

MUM. I'll pop a couple of hundred in your account. You're my favourite after all.

SAGE. Mum, you can't say that!

MUM. Well, you are! Of course you are. You're old enough now to not be weird about it... Oh don't look at me like that. I should've stopped at you really. You did get the best of me.

SAGE. I've got my dad's nose.

MUM. You're right. It's a horrible nose. Ugly. I'm just telling the truth.

SAGE. Get off the chair and stop showing off.

MUM. Darling, when I'm gone /

SAGE. Mum, you're not /

MUM. Not the cancer. I've beaten that already, I can feel it. But it made me think: when I go, you kids will try and get on, won't you? You will make sure of that?

The memory fades. We are back in the present where the SISTERS *are fighting.*

The doorbell rings.

DERREN (*offstage*). Granny's here!

SAGE. Alright. Everyone on your best behaviour! Acknowledgement?

ALL. Acknowledgment.

STORM. We're not finished here.

GRANNY *and* LARA *enter.*

'Symphony No. 83 in G Minor, Hob 1:83 "La paule":
I. Allegro spiritoso' by Franz Joseph Haydn plays.

Chapter Four – Dinner

Projection: 'Granny (Dawn Pelican) 1929'.

GRANNY. Dawn, Dawn meaning the first light in the morning, or the beginning of a phenomenon or period of time, was born Dawn Grant in October 1929. As American investors jumped from tall New York buildings, I came into the world premature and killed my mother in the process. In 1950, I married my husband and in 1953, we bought our first house for:

Projection: '£1,891'.

When a pint of milk cost:

Projection: '£0.05'.

The Prime Minister was:

Projection: Photo of Sir Winston Churchill.

And the Queen looked like:

Projection: Photo from the Queen's coronation.

A few months later, Rosemary was born.

MAYA *enters.*

MAYA. Hey, Granny!

GRANNY. Hello, love.

MAYA. Gran, there's a special someone I want you to meet!

GRANNY. Oooooooh.

STORM *enters.*

STORM. Hi, Granny.

GRANNY. My little Storm in a teacup!

JOY *enters.*

JOY. Glad you could make it.

GRANNY. Of course!

DODO *enters.*

MAYA. This is my boyfriend Dodo.

DODO. You are so beautiful, aren't you?

GRANNY. Are you Maya's boyfriend? Can you be my boyfriend too?

DODO. Oh yes please! Wow, what a woman!

SAGE *enters.*

SAGE. Hey, Granny!

GRANNY. Rosemary, dear…

SAGE. Oh no, Granny.

STORM. That's Sage.

GRANNY. Of course. I know that. You look different /

SAGE. Oh it's my hair. I'm growing it out.

GRANNY. How's your friend?

SAGE. She's dead to me, Granny.

Little awkward pause. DERREN *enters.*

DERREN. Okay, grub's up! Everyone serve yourself.

All sit.

SAGE. Oh wait – before everyone eats I just want to remind everyone that this is a meal for Mum! So eat and drink as she would!

MAYA. What, down two bottles of red, and dance on the table?

SAGE. No, Maya, savour every bite. Enjoy!

MAYA. Blue skies to Dodo and Derren for making dinner.

SAGE/STORM/MAYA/JOY/GRANNY. Blue skies!

DERREN. We didn't really make the dinner. We just heated it up and put it on plates.

DODO. I made the baba ganoush and the couscous salad.

MAYA. Oh my god. Everyone has to try his baba ganoush!

JOY. Not for me, thanks.

MAYA. He made it himself.

DODO. From scratch!

JOY. Maybe later.

MAYA. It's so good!

DODO. Tahini and eggplant.

MAYA. That means aubergine.

JOY. No thank you!

SAGE. Have we got any sriracha?

STORM. We've run out.

MAYA. Granny looks older than I remember.

JOY. She's in her nineties.

SAGE. Shut up!

DODO. Who's bought all this delicious wine?

DERREN. Oh don't worry about it.

DODO. Oh come on. Let me transfer you the money. Do you
    have a Monzo card?

JOY. Thanks, Dodo, but it's alright.

MAYA. It looks like she might break. Freaks me out.

JOY. She's still Granny.

MAYA. Is she?

SAGE. Is that a whole ham?

DERREN. What's wrong with ham?

SAGE. Mum didn't eat ham.

DERREN. It's from Waitrose.

SAGE. But it's Mum's meal and she wouldn't have eaten it.

JOY. It's fine!

DODO. You got everything you need there, Grandma?

GRANNY. Where's Lara's plate?

MAYA. Who?

GRANNY. Lara. My friend.

They all look up and notice LARA. *All at once: 'Oh gosh I'm
so sorry', 'Hi Lara, how are you?', 'Of course', 'Have some
of my potatoes', 'Didn't see you there!', 'Do you like carrots?'*

STORM *brings in a chair for* LARA. *She sits. They eat in silence.*

DERREN. Can you pass the carrots?

STORM. Sure.

DODO. Grandma, would you like to try a bit of my baba ganoush?

GRANNY. Err…

DODO. There you go.

DERREN. Sage, how's the exhibition coming along?

SAGE. Pretty good.

DERREN. We loved your last one, didn't we, Joy? It was so cerebral! Especially that one with the, the, the…

SAGE. The Flag Room?

DERREN. No, no the… which one was it, Joy?

JOY. The Rock Circle.

DERREN. Yeah! The Rock Circle. It was beautiful.

SAGE. I didn't think it would be your thing.

DERREN. Why not?

SAGE. It's just a bit. You know, out there.

DERREN. I can be 'out there'.

SAGE. Ha! Derren. You live in Swindon.

DERREN. What's Swindon got to do with it?

JOY. Don't take the bait.

MAYA. How's the new stuff?

SAGE. I don't know, I just think maybe since Mum died my work has gotten really shit.

MAYA. Don't say that.

SAGE. Or maybe it's better I don't know. Maybe more urgent or something.

DODO. Ooh, could you paint a portrait of me and Maya in the style of Gustav Klimt's *The Kiss*?

SAGE. I don't really do portraits.

DODO. I could pay you, obviously.

SAGE. No.

STORM. Maya, are you having seconds?

MAYA. Uh yeah.

STORM. I don't think we decided /

MAYA. Well, I decided that now.

STORM. Lara didn't even get a full plate.

LARA. Oh, no it's fine.

STORM. There won't be enough to go around.

LARA. It's okay! I've had plenty.

STORM. You're not thinking of other people.

DERREN. I've really had enough too.

STORM. I was hoping to save some for leftovers.

MAYA. I need my energy.

DODO. She does need her energy.

JOY. What does that mean?

STORM. I'm so sorry, Lara. I'm so sorry that we haven't thought about what *you* might need.

LARA. Oh no, it's fine.

STORM. It may be fine, Lara. But is it fair?

Silence.

SAGE. So, how old are you, Dodo?

DODO. Thank you for asking, Sage. It's interesting, I honestly don't think I know any more.

Silence.

GRANNY. Can I have some ham?

DERREN. Oh absolutely!

GRANNY. Where's it from?

DERREN. Waitrose.

GRANNY. I love Waitrose.

SAGE. Actually, Derren, a big impulse for making the Rock Circle was thinking about Mum. And the choices she made in her life. She was spot-on most of the time, but I've never understood why she had so many kids.

JOY. What do you mean?

SAGE. Well she was an 'eco-warrior', but she popped us out like ping pong balls!

JOY. Sage!

SAGE. I just think we should all face up to the fact that having babies nowadays equates to some serious moral fuckuppery.

STORM. She's right.

DERREN. What, everyone should just stop making babies?

SAGE. Derren, this planet is in danger and – pass the hummus – one way that /

MAYA. Mum had as many kids as she wanted, and I don't think anyone else is allowed to say otherwise. That's her choice as a woman. That's her right.

DODO. That's right, baby.

JOY. Can we not talk about this, please?

MAYA. Childbirth is a human right.

DERREN. Alright, alright, this isn't something we want to talk about over Dodo's baba ganoush.

MAYA. It's my right to have a child. It's my legacy. The legacy of this family.

SAGE. Ha! Maya with a baby! Can you imagine?

MAYA. Well, maybe you won't have to imagine!!

STORM. What does that mean?

She can't get the words out. She mumbles.

MAYA. Well, mmm, prrr-nat.

JOY. What? What are you saying?

MAYA. Um pregn-nart.

DERREN. Wait, what's happening?

MAYA. Dodo and I, er experk-tn.

ALL. WHAAAT?

MAYA. I'm having a baby! I'm pregnant alright?!

Silence.

DODO. Woohoo!

JOY. Is this true?

MAYA. Yes.

SAGE. Actually true?

MAYA. Yes.

SAGE. Jesus. Congratulations.

MAYA. Thank you.

DODO. Thank you.

The SISTERS *look at* JOY. JOY *stands.*

STORM. Joy?

JOY. We're fucked. This family is officially fucked. One barren, one lesbian.

SAGE. Hey.

JOY. One completely unfuckable.

STORM. Hey!

JOY. Now our last chance of carrying on the family bloodline has been hijacked by some idiot Yank you met at a mindfulness retreat.

MAYA. Don't you dare talk about my boyfriend like that.

JOY. Don't get knocked up by a stranger.

MAYA. Don't be a cow.

JOY. You're a child, Maya. What makes you think you can bring up another human being? And you're trying to do it with that dipshit over there!

DODO. My name is Dodo.

JOY. Oh, Maya, grow up!

The SISTERS fight through gesture and sound. Warfare. They slip into slow motion.

GRANNY. I could never have imagined giving birth to such a family. To such a group of people. Look at them. Look at the way they move. All of this, through me. Through my daughter, my granddaughters. Same blood. Very. Different. Life. Carrying this blood, into what? Into heaven knows what. Tearing each other apart.

We burst back into reality.

JOY. Sorry, Dodo. I'm sorry.

DERREN rises from his chair.

I'm fine.

JOY leaves. DERREN follows her.

MAYA. I'm sorry I didn't tell you in a more constructive way.

MAYA leaves.

STORM. I think I made some really important points in my presentation and no one is talking about it.

SAGE. This is not the time, Storm!

SAGE *leaves*. STORM *leaves*.

DODO. Nobody's even touched the couscous salad.

DODO *leaves*.

Maya! Hey, Maya!

GRANNY. Lara. Leave, love.

LARA. I've got to stay to put you to bed, Dawn.

GRANNY. Oh don't be ridiculous.

LARA. I'm here to look after you.

GRANNY. I pay your wages, Lara. Leave.

LARA (*to* DERREN). Is that alright with you?

DERREN *nods*.

(*To* GRANNY.) I'll pick you up in the morning!

GRANNY. Piss off, Lara.

LARA *leaves*.

You've got a lovely beard. Bushy. Like a badger. Are you okay, Derren?

DERREN. Not feeling my best, if I'm honest with you, Granny.

GRANNY. Me neither. Baby Maya with a baby.

DERREN. I didn't think you'd heard that, Granny.

GRANNY. I'm sorry, Derren. But a great-grandmother! No one should be made to feel that old. It's desperately unflattering. Derren, I want to leave now.

DERREN. I thought you said you wanted to stay, Granny.

GRANNY. I want to die.

DERREN. Oh. You don't mean that, Granny.

GRANNY. Kill me, Derren.

DERREN. Oh, no, Granny.

GRANNY. I tried to jump out the window. But I forgot I lived on the ground floor.

DERREN. No, Granny.

GRANNY. Do you know how much I cost?

DERREN. That doesn't matter.

GRANNY. My nursing home isn't cheap.

DERREN. We love having you here, Granny.

GRANNY. I live in pain, it hurts to breathe, I can't hear, I can't dance, I can't do anything I like.

DERREN. Oh, Granny.

GRANNY. It's not the only road, Derren. You and Joy should consider yourselves lucky. It's painful having children. It's painful losing them too.

DERREN. I'm sure it is, Granny.

GRANNY. Shall we have a glass of sherry?

'Symphony No. 45 in F-Sharp Minor "Farewell": IV. Finale: Presto – Adagio' by Franz Joseph Haydn plays.

Chapter Five – Therapy

JOY*'s memory.* MUM *is played by* MAYA.

JOY. Anyway he didn't keep the ring in the house because he knows I would have found it so he gave the ring to our friend Chris who had to meet us in a café where we were having brunch. But he knew I'd twig if I saw him so he hid him in the toilet.

MUM *enters.*

MUM. Derren hid in the toilet?!

JOY. No, not Derren. Chris hid in the toilet with the ring. Are you even listening?

MUM. Yes, yes sorry it's quite a long story.

JOY. Don't worry about it then.

MUM. No, don't be like that.

JOY. What's the point, you're not listening.

MUM. I am! Please tell me. Leamington, Chris hid in the toilet, brunch...

JOY. Okay fine. We went for a walk and he got down on one knee by the river.

MUM. Awww that's nice.

Pause.

JOY. Go on then.

MUM. What?

JOY. I know what you're thinking so you might as well just say it.

MUM. I'm thinking that all sounds nice. You know I love Derren as much as the next mum. Derren's wonderful.

JOY. Mum /

MUM. It's your decision.

JOY. Yeah it is. We thought we should do it now, soon. You know, give us something for us all to look forward to /

MUM. Before I kick the bucket, you mean. I'm not dead yet!

JOY. I didn't mean it like /

MUM. Joy, my darling. You need to remember that the convention of marriage is a capitalist, misogynist construct... But whatever makes you happy!

Anyway, I'm going out tonight. I managed to seduce one of the nurses from radiology, I might have done something naughty in the cleaning closet.

JOY. Jesus.

MUM. I gave him a handjob.

JOY. Urgh.

MUM. She's still got it!

She leaves. The memory fades. Everyone is in the room, not talking to one another. DERREN *goes to hug* JOY. MAYA *enters.*

DODO. Okay, I've been sensing a lot of negative energy in here. And I'd like us to start talking about it, okay?

Let's start by shaking it out. Maya, c'mon, you know this one. Shake it out. Imagine that there's a bit of bubble gum stuck on the end of your fingers, you're trying to shake it off. Both hands. And then woosah! Up in to the cosmos.

Right, now that we're a little looser. Derren. Come with me, Derren. Come on, Derren!

DERREN *and* DODO *exit, a few seconds later they re-enter with a table and some household objects.*

Just down there… Thank you so much, Derren.

Now, we are going to use these household objects to talk about our feelings. So you pick one up. And you say, 'This is Dodo. Dodo is feeling like there is a lot of negative energy in this room.' Except you don't say Dodo, you say your own name, and you talk about your own feelings. Okay?

And then the other objects can represent the other people in your life. Who would like to go first?

JOY. I'll go.

DODO. Great.

JOY *picks up an object.*

JOY. Imagine this is Joy.

DODO. You don't actually have to say 'imagine'.

JOY. Imagine this is Joy.

DODO. Whatever works for you.

JOY puppets the objects.

JOY. Joy is sad that Mum is gone. And when everyone gets together, it gets really loud. And Joy doesn't like that. At the moment, Joy has been going through some stuff and she loves you all very much, obviously.

JOY puts the objects back on the table.

DODO. That was so beautiful. Thank you, Joy. Who would like to go next?

DERREN gets up to reassure JOY.

Derren?

DERREN. No thanks, mate.

SAGE holds STORM's hand, smiles, squeezes.

SAGE. Come on.

STORM doesn't move. SAGE encourages STORM to go up.

STORM. I'll go.

DODO. Great.

STORM moves the objects away, leaving two on the table. She picks up a remaining object.

STORM. This is Storm.

She picks up another.

This is Mum.

She gestures to a space beside her.

This is Storm's future.

She puppets the STORM and Mum objects.

Do what you want with your life. I can look after myself.

Okay, Mum. I'm going to move away.

Hey, Storm, it's my chemo tomorrow. Joy is working, and she's busy trying to start her own family. Sage has got her big exhibition coming up. Maya is in Mexico. Can you take me to the hospital?

Okay, Mum. I'll be right there.

Oh, I feel a lot weaker than I expected.

That's okay, Mum. I'll stay the night.

Night, Storm.

Night, Mum.

I've thrown up.

Okay, Mum. I'll be right in.

Hey, Storm, I've fainted in Tesco. Can you help?

Okay, Mum.

Hey, Storm, I'm not eating.

Oh.

And don't tell Sage, she's busy. I don't want to worry her.

Okay, Mum. By the way, Joy will be over this weekend. And I'm so glad. She gives me some time. I am so grateful to her. She has such good intentions. But Joy doesn't ask me what I want. She says, 'Storm, go out with your friends.' But I don't have any friends. They've all moved away. So I go to the pub and I just sit there in the corner and all I'm thinking about is if Mum's okay.

Hey, Storm, it's got into my brain. I can't remember who you are.

Oh.

I'm dead now.

STORM *puts the Mum puppet down.*

That's really hard. That you're dead now.

I didn't do it for the money. I just thought that in the shittest moments, that it would be worth something. That what I put in, would be paid back somehow. And I know, it was my choice to stay, and that you don't owe me anything. But I'm so tired, I've spent so long in this fucking house, and the world is so terrifying to me now.

JOY *and* MAYA *hug* STORM. SAGE *plugs her phone into the sound system, she finds Grace Jones. They do the dance, all together this time. Doorbell rings. They keep dancing.* DERREN *answers the door.* LUKE *enters.*

LUKE. Alright.

JOY *turns the music off.*

Surprise.

SAGE. Luke!

LUKE. Sage.

SAGE. Thought you weren't coming.

LUKE. Well, I saw Maya's Instagram story so thought I'd swing by.

SAGE. You knew about this.

LUKE. Knew about what?

JOY. Don't play dumb, Luke. Storm told you this was happening.

LUKE. What was happening?

JOY. I don't want to play this game.

LUKE. What game?

DODO. Sorry, who is this guy?

MAYA. Our baby brother, Luke.

DODO. A brother? What a wonderful surprise, so pleased to meet you.

LUKE. Who's this?

SAGE. Maya's new boyfriend.

DODO. Life partner.

LUKE. Okay.

DODO. Okay!

LUKE. Wait, why was I not invited?

SAGE. What?

LUKE. Mum's birthday. Why was I not invited?

SAGE. You were.

STORM. I didn't tell him.

JOY. You didn't tell him?

STORM. I didn't tell him, okay?

JOY. Storm.

MAYA. Did you forget?

STORM. No, Maya, I didn't forget. I didn't want him here.

LUKE. What?!

MAYA. Please don't get angry.

LUKE. I'm allowed to get angry.

MAYA. I know, sweetheart, but it's not nice.

LUKE. You're not fucking nice.

JOY. Luke! Please. Is there a way of us doing this without
    getting mad at each other?

LUKE. Why didn't she ask me to come?

STORM. I…

SAGE. Storm?

STORM. I just /

LUKE. You just…?

STORM. I just didn't want you to do this, okay? We're talking about the will, alright.

We're talking about Mum's will and I just wanted to have this conversation in peace and quiet and I didn't want to have to deal with you behaving like a spoilt brat. You never came to Mum's birthdays anyway.

LUKE. Fuck you!

JOY. Hey! Martin may let you get away with it but you do not talk like that in this house.

LUKE. Sorry.

JOY. Not in this house.

LUKE. Sorry.

JOY. Thank you.

Pause.

STORM. Okay. Luke, do you want to be part of this discussion?

LUKE. Yes.

STORM. Well, we've just decided to split a portion of Mum's inheritance to compensate me for the time I spent caring for her.

JOY. No we didn't.

STORM. I thought… I thought we'd…

SAGE. Tomorrow, Storm.

STORM. No. We have to deal with this now. We have to. The solicitor is coming first thing tomorrow morning. Luke, what do you think?

LUKE. Now you care about what I think?

STORM. Luke, seriously! What do you think?

LUKE. Keep the money, give it to Africa, I don't give a shit.

STORM. Right, so he's on board!

SAGE. I don't want to talk about this any more.

STORM. But /

SAGE. You don't get to make the decisions about what we do.
You lied about Luke, and Pelicans don't lie.

STORM. But I /

SAGE. No. Not tonight, Storm. It's Mum's birthday. We're here
for her.

STORM. No we're not. We're here for you! We're here for you,
Sage.

SAGE scoffs.

Why else would we be here? You were so insistent that we
all get together for this ridiculous morbid ritual. But as soon
as there's something important to discuss, I'm the one being
ridiculous.

SAGE. We all wanted to come... right?

STORM storms out. Silence. JOY goes to comfort SAGE.

No! In T minus two hours and thirteen minutes, we are all
going to go upstairs and eat cake on Mum's bed, just like the
old days.

MAYA puts on 'We Are Family' by Sister Sledge.

Thank you, Maya!

JOY. Right, I'm going to get smashed. Shit prosecco, anyone?

LUKE. Yes.

SAGE. Me too!

JOY goes to leave.

MAYA. Yeah, me three!

JOY. Are you kidding me?

JOY and SAGE leave. STORM follows.

DODO. Maya, you are not having any prosecco.

MAYA. It's one sip for Mum! It's fine.

DODO. Your body is a literal temple for our unborn child.

MAYA. Dodo, it's fine.

DODO. That is a big no-no for our little Dodo.

MAYA. Don't touch me!

LUKE. Wait, Maya's having a baby? Maya, are you having a baby?

DODO. Yup.

LUKE. With this guy?

DODO. Yeah.

LUKE. Congratulations. Welcome to the family.

DODO. Thanks, you're gonna be an uncle!

LUKE. Mate, Mum would have loved you. Maya, wouldn't Mum have loved this guy?

DODO. Hey, man, are you mocking me?

MAYA's memory. MUM *is played by* SAGE.

MUM *enters on the phone.*

MUM. Martin. Martin. What did he steal from Tesco? Well, I can't be there every minute of the day. Martin, he's your son as well. Martin! Martin?

She hangs up and screams into the phone.

It never ends!

MUM *lies down on the floor.*

I am so tired.

MAYA *joins her on the floor.*

There were so many things I wanted to do.

She stands.

Promise me you'll never have kids… Drink?

MUM *exits. The memory fades.*

DODO *and* LUKE *are mid-argument.*

LUKE. So we're going to be brothers, yeah?

MAYA. Leave him alone, Luke.

LUKE. I'm just being friendly.

DODO. Are you okay?

MAYA. Not now!

DERREN *approaches* LUKE.

DERREN. How've you been anyway, mate?

LUKE. Fine.

DERREN. Still at college?

LUKE. Yeah.

DERREN. Still got your video-diary thing going?

LUKE. Joy said you and her can't have kids.

DERREN. Oh. Right. When did she tell you that?

LUKE. WhatsApp.

DERREN. Oh right. Well, you know, we've not been trying all that long so I reckon it'll be fine to be honest.

DODO. Have you tried matcha tea?

DERREN. What?

DODO. Matcha tea. I could make you an herbal blend, might help with the ol' potency problem.

DERREN. No.

DODO. Oh I just / thought that.

SAGE *and* JOY *enter with drinks.*

SAGE. Okay, we have twelve bottles of cheap prosecco in the kitchen that need drinking.

So, Mum, if you're up there, please grant us the strength to drink as much of it as is humanly possible. Thank you! Swindon, dancefloor.

JOY. Come on, babe, let's dance! It'll be fun.

DERREN. I'm not quite there yet.

SAGE. Go on, Swindon, give the girl a dance!

JOY. Come on, Swindon!

DERREN. Are you kidding me?

>   DERREN *exits*.

JOY. Derren, what's the matter?

>   JOY *exits*.

SAGE. The cake. I need to decorate the cake!

>   SAGE *exits*.

DODO. Hey, bro, I feel like we got off on the wrong foot back there, let's start over, let's rewind. Hi my name is Dodo by the way.

LUKE. My name is Gogo the fuck awayway.

>   MAYA *laughs*.

DODO. Dodo taking five.

>   DODO *exits*.

LUKE. Congratulations.

MAYA. Thanks.

LUKE. I'm gonna be an uncle.

MAYA. Yeah you are.

LUKE. That's cool.

MAYA. Yeah?

LUKE. Yeah. I think this baby could be good for us. This time next year we'll all be back here. But we'll have a baby to play with. And we can teach it whatever we want. I can tell it about the Marvel Universe and you can tell it about all the places you've been.

MAYA. We're selling the house, Luke.

LUKE. I know, but...

MUM *walks through the room.*

GRANNY. Rosemary?

MAYA. No, Granny.

GRANNY. Rosemary?

LUKE. She's gone.

GRANNY. No she hasn't. Can you take me to the toilet?

SAGE, GRANNY *and* LUKE *exit.* STORM *enters through the door.*

Chapter Six – In the Dead of the Night

STORM *in the garden.* DODO *enters.*

DODO. Hey, what are you doing out here?

STORM. Family. I just needed some fresh air.

DODO. Yeah, I hear ya. Luke is a hoot. I didn't even know you guys had a brother, so...

STORM. Sometimes it's better not to talk about him. Sometimes it's better to just let him be.

DODO. I'm sure he's a nice guy deep down.

STORM. You didn't have to live with him. I couldn't bring friends home because he would take stuff from their bags. We had to put locks on our bedroom doors. When Mum got ill, he just pissed off to his dad's. Didn't even visit.

DODO. I'm sorry.

MAYA *as* MUM *enters.*

STORM. You know, I used to pretend this end of the garden was a whole other country. I'd get in my plane, like this, neaaaaaaooow, and end up here in less than two seconds. Bit cheaper than EasyJet.

DODO. I'm sure. So, where are you now?

STORM. Hawaii.

DODO. Nice. Fancy.

STORM. Hot.

DODO *gets in his plane.*

DODO. Neaaaaaaooow. Seeking permission to land in Hawaii.

STORM. Permission granted.

He lands.

Aloha.

DODO (*in Southern US accent*). Why hello there, ma'am. Do you come here often?

STORM. All the time.

DODO. Would you like to try some magic mushrooms?

STORM. No. What?

DODO. Okay, sorry.

She goes to leave.

STORM. My system is very sensitive to stimulants of any kind.

DODO. It's okay, you don't have to take them.

STORM. What's it like?

MUM. Stormy, dinner time! Come back from Hawaii please.

STORM, DODO *and* MAYA *as* MUM *exit. Back inside,* SAGE *and* DERREN *enter.*

SAGE. It's half eleven. Where is everyone?

DERREN. I dunno.

SAGE. So much for everyone being together for Mum's birthday – (*Shouts offstage*.) Pelicans assemble! Pelicaaaaaans!

DERREN. Sage, Sage. Could you just not, please.

SAGE. Is Swindon a little grumpy?

DERREN. No, I'm not grumpy.

SAGE. Is Swindon man throwing his toys out of the Swindon pram?

DERREN. Can you just stop?

SAGE. Swindon angry. Swindon smash.

DERREN. Stop, okay, stop with the Swindon thing. I actually like Swindon, I like my life.

SAGE. Derren.

DERREN. It just really pisses me off.

SAGE. Derren.

DERREN. When you're all here… You know you lot, you're just not nice…

SAGE. It's all part of the charm.

DERREN. Well, it's not charming. It isn't. Joy's suffering. She's really suffering and nobody cares.

    JOY *enters with a bottle of prosecco*.

JOY. Where have you been?

DERREN. In the car.

JOY. Why?

DERREN. I needed some air.

JOY. Do you feel better?

DERREN. What's that supposed to mean?

JOY. Oh that's great. I'm fine.

DERREN. Well, you don't sound fine.

JOY. Oh really? I wonder why that could be?!

DERREN. We aren't doing this now /

JOY. Yes we are /

DERREN. No we aren't /

JOY. Yes we are!

DERREN. No, we're not! We're supposed to be on the same team.

Pause.

JOY. Well, this team doesn't seem to be doing very well at the moment, does it?

And some teams seem to be winning without even trying and that's not fair!

Pause.

Well? Anything to say on that?

DERREN. What do you want me to say?

JOY. Anything. Scream. Shout. Swear. Throw something.

DERREN. I don't know what to do. I don't know what you want me to do.

MAYA, LUKE *and* GRANNY *enter.*

MAYA. Marry Linford Christie, kill Noel Edmonds, shag Phil Mitchell.

LUKE. Shag Phil Mitchell?! Are you kidding?

DERREN *exits.* JOY *pours herself a large glass of wine.*

MAYA. He's got something about him. He's manly!

GRANNY. I'd give him one!

LUKE. Gross.

MAYA. Right, Sage. Margaret Thatcher, Hyacinth Bucket, Dot Cotton.

SAGE. Easy. Kill Hyacinth Bucket.

MAYA. Interesting.

SAGE. Marry Dot Cotton, shag Thatcher.

MAYA. You're kidding.

SAGE. She might be Satan but I bet she wouldn't mess around in the sack.

MAYA. Fair enough. What about you, Luke?

LUKE. I don't know who any of those people are.

'Oh come on, I don't', etc., while SAGE *chooses a record – 'Imagine' by John Lennon. When it starts playing, they stop.*

SAGE. What?

LUKE. Are you kidding me?

SAGE. What?

MAYA. All those records and you pick this?

SAGE. Yes, and?

LUKE. And it's boring.

SAGE. It's not boring, it's the most important song of all time. Listen to it.

LUKE. We've already listened to it, about a thousand times.

SAGE. Fine, you might have been listening but you haven't been hearing. Actually listen to the words. It's a manifesto. It's a set of ideas.

LUKE. I know the words, we know every single word, just like the rest of the world.

How old is this song now, like a hundred years old?

MAYA. Like fifty years old.

LUKE. Fifty years old. Hasn't really worked then has it? If it had, surely we'd all be hippies by now, running around in fields throwing flowers about.

MAYA. Didn't he abuse his wife?

SAGE. I don't /

GRANNY. He gave money to the IRA.

LUKE. That's not very peaceful.

MAYA. I heard he had a refrigerated wardrobe to keep his fur coats in.

LUKE. See? Hypocrite! I get in trouble all the time for sitting around imagining stuff but never actually doing anything.

SAGE. It's not naive to imagine a better world and strive towards making it.

LUKE. Oh yeah, hello, I'm John Lennon. Imagine this, imagine that, wouldn't it be great if there was no war and we all shared everything and everyone just got off with each other all the time.

SAGE. This was Mum's favourite song. So stop being a cynical prick and stop saying snarky shit about things that meant stuff to Mum and mean stuff to me.

LUKE. It's true. The song's bullshit.

SAGE. I don't care! Maybe the song is shit and John Lennon was a prick, but there is value in the things Mum believed in.

LUKE. Like what?

SAGE. Love, understanding. That we can work it out. That we can work together.

That the world can be a family, that humanity is good.

LUKE. Humanity is good? You think humanity is good? When the Prime Minister looks like this.

Projection: Photo of Boris Johnson.

And the Queen looks like this.

Projection: Photo of the Queen.

Why have we even got a Royal Family? Look how fucking old she is!

And all Mum could ever do is sit on the sidelines and complain. She was sitting on a house worth this.

Projection: '£229,431'.

If she actually wanted to make a difference aren't there better things she could've done with that money than just leave it to us?

JOY. Luke!

LUKE. What? And what's going to happen to you, now Mum's not around to buy your sculptures?

SAGE. You wouldn't dare talk like this if she was here.

LUKE. If you follow the bible of Mum, you end up with Sage: sofa-surfing in South East London, 'working' in her 'studio', but still somehow having the moral high ground? Bollocks. Mum was an idiot and a hypocrite and so is she.

SAGE. You know I wish there was some reason that you're such a dick. But from where I'm standing turns out you're just a dick. You're like a real dick, like a full dick.

LUKE. What, you think it was easy growing up in this house with you lot?

SAGE. Yes, yes it was. It was the easiest. We could do whatever we wanted.

LUKE. You could do whatever you wanted. Whenever I did anything I wanted, Mum would just lecture me about my place in the wider story of my gender, and then cry. When you lot do that, when you cry, we stop having a conversation and I can't win.

MAYA. It's not about winning, Luke.

LUKE. Then why do you lot always win?

SAGE. Grow up.

LUKE. Me grow up?

SAGE. Yeah.

LUKE. Sage wants Luke to grow up?

SAGE. Yes, grow up.

LUKE *recites the first line of 'Imagine'.*

Luke.

He continues with the second.

Stop it.

And the third.

Shut. The. Fuck. Up.

He begins the chorus and then picks up the record.

SAGE *is crying.*

JOY. That's enough!

LUKE. Look, look at what you're doing.

SAGE. I'm not trying to cry, you idiot.

She leaves. JOY *follows.*

MAYA. Strong decision, Luke.

LUKE. Well, at least I didn't get knocked up by my yoga teacher.

MAYA. Thanks, mate. Come on, Granny.

MAYA *goes to leave with* GRANNY.

GRANNY. No, leave me with him.

MAYA *leaves.*

GRANNY*'s wheelchair starts to roll downstage.*

Errrrrrrr.

LUKE *rescues her.*

Thank you.

LUKE. Sorry, Gran.

LUKE *goes to leave.*

GRANNY. Going somewhere?

LUKE. Home.

GRANNY. It's almost midnight.

LUKE. I'm not staying here. This family is fucked.

GRANNY. Yes. And?

LUKE. And I'm leaving.

GRANNY. Coward.

LUKE. Whatever.

GRANNY. You're just like your mother, so hot-headed.

LUKE. No I'm not.

GRANNY. Yes you are.

LUKE. Well, I don't give a shit.

GRANNY. Yes, you do. And stop cursing so much, it makes you sound stupid.

LUKE. I am stupid.

GRANNY. No you're not /

LUKE. I'm a stupid idiot!

GRANNY. No you're not.

LUKE. I'm a dickhead.

GRANNY. Stop wallowing and come and give your granny a cuddle.

LUKE. No.

GRANNY. Give your granny a cuddle.

LUKE *hugs* GRANNY. YOUNG GRANNY *enters*.

Why do you hold yourself in such low regard? Nobody else does.

LUKE. Yeah they do.

GRANNY. No they don't. They've just come to expect certain things of you. Why not prove them wrong? Show them you're a Pelican.

LUKE. I'm not a Pelican, I'm a Fletcher.

GRANNY. You're very much a Pelican. Come on now, love. Time to buck up. What would your mother say?

LUKE. Pull your tits up.

GRANNY. That's it.

LUKE. I don't need my mum to live my life.

GRANNY. Go on!

LUKE. We're Peli-cans, not Peli-can'ts!

GRANNY. Quite right. Quite right. Go on then, love…

LUKE *stands*.

Projection: 'Luke 2002'.

LUKE. Luke. From the Latin *Lucius* meaning the bright one, was born on 20th July 2002. I came into the world quietly, barely even a whimper. When I arrived I fell asleep, and I stayed that way for basically the next two weeks. Everyone that came to see me would say the same thing. Lovely baby. Really lovely baby. Luke.

GRANNY. Well done. Pop one of your tunes on then.

LUKE *puts on 'Dreaming' by S.P. Y.*

What's this one called?

LUKE. Liquid, Gran.

GRANNY. Pardon?

LUKE. Liquid drum and bass.

GRANNY. Liquid?

LUKE. Yes.

GRANNY. Why liquid?

LUKE. I don't know, Granny. Are you tapping your toe there, Granny?

GRANNY. Yes.

LUKE. Are you dancing?

GRANNY. I believe I am.

LUKE. Go on, Granny!

LUKE *starts to push* GRANNY*'s wheelchair in a circle, getting faster and faster.*

GRANNY. Turn up it up then. Turn up the liquid bass!

LUKE. Go on, Granny!

LUKE *exits with* GRANNY *in wheelchair.* YOUNG GRANNY *dances.*

Two MUMS *appear and circle* GRANNY.

DODO *and* STORM *are in the garden.*

GRANNY *stays dancing in slow motion.*

DODO. Your garden is… so beautiful.

STORM. It was. I haven't really had time to… It's got a bit messy.

DODO. Everything is breathing.

STORM. I don't think it's affecting me at all, I just feel really normal.

DODO. Yeah. These flowers over here…

STORM. The tulips. You know tulips used to be super-valuable. Back in the 1600s or something, their price went up so much you could buy a whole house with a tulip bulb.

DODO. Whoa...

STORM. I used to think it was all made up, money and the market and deals and transactions, but now I've grown up and realised that it's literally all there is.

There's no point fighting it.

You and Maya are having a baby together. That's crazy. I mean you don't know each other all that well...

DODO. Sure we do.

STORM. Do you love her?

DODO. Yeah.

STORM. Well, you must really think she's a future worth investing in. Do you think she'll give you good returns? Do you value her?

DODO. Yes I do.

STORM. How much?

DODO. How m–

STORM. Yes but literally how much? In pounds and pence. A thousand pounds, ten thousand pounds, a million even?

They look into each other's eyes.

DODO. Storm, there are so many things in this world that money cannot buy... Human connectedness... Emotional honesty... Flowers...

STORM. You can definitely buy flowers.

DODO. I'd buy you a flower.

She kisses him. He lets her.

STORM. Oh god. This is actually happening, isn't it.

DODO. Yep.

STORM. Oh god.

MAYA appears in another space and walks between them.

MAYA and DODO kiss again.

DODO. Don't tell Maya.

DODO and STORM exit as DERREN enters.

We are back inside.

DERREN. All a bit much?

MAYA. Yes. All a bit much.

DERREN. I don't have a big family. I envy that. All that energy.
Even Granny!… Can you feel it yet?

MAYA. What? Oh, no.

DERREN. Do you mind if I touch it?

*He moves closer to MAYA as if to touch her belly. She draws
back.*

Oh, shit. Sorry. That's was weird. I just wanted to –
Congratulations.

MAYA. Congratulations… for what? Well done, Maya, your
life is over. Congratulations on your little bundle of cells.
Good on you, Dodo, for planting that seed in her. God he's
so damn proud of himself too, like he has set up basecamp in
my belly. He keeps touching it, there's nothing even there
yet. Is this it? Is this gonna be it for the next seven months?!

JOY, STORM and SAGE enter as MUMS.

Two years? For the rest of my life? Because no amount of
fucking meditation is gonna get me through this.

I'm scared. I can't go to Joy, not this time. I just need my
mum. I need her to tell me it's all alright. That I can do this,
cos I'm not sure I can.

DERREN. Maya…

MAYA. Oh. Go on then.

DERREN. I feel a bit uncomfortable about it now to be honest.

MAYA. Do it.

DERREN. No.

MAYA. Touch my fucking belly, Derren.

DERREN. Okay.

He touches it. He stays too long. He kneels. He presses his ear to her belly. The three MUMS *go over to* MAYA *and brush her hair.*

MAYA. You know how to be quiet.

DERREN. Uhh.

MAYA. Dodo is always talking.

DERREN. You can do this, Maya.

MUMS exit.

Oh. I think it's kicking.

MAYA. Derren, it's the size of a butterbean! It definitely isn't kicking.

He stays. JOY *enters and sees this image.* DERREN *sees* JOY, *gets up.*

JOY. Sorry to interrupt. Derren, is there any more prosecco?

MAYA. I'll get it.

DERREN. No, it's alright. I'll just… I'll leave you guys to it.

DERREN exits.

MAYA. Joy.

JOY. Maya.

How did you do it?

MAYA. I dunno, we just /

JOY. How did you do it? Because we've tried everything. I've been on the Mediterranean diet for three years. We've spent seventeen grand on IVF. Not to mention the bloating, the cramps and the vaginal scans. They're painful. I've stopped wearing nail polish.

MAYA. What? Why?

JOY. The fumes. I dunno.

MAYA. Joy, I'm sorry.

JOY. Meehhhh.

MAYA. You can see it whenever you like.

JOY. Careful, might not give it back.

MAYA. I'm scared, Joy.

JOY. Your life doesn't have to change, Maya, it doesn't. Thirty.

MAYA. What?

JOY. Thirty grand.

MAYA. What?

JOY. Okay, forty, not a penny more. Call it fifty but that's my final offer, I can't go any higher.

MAYA. Stop playing around. It's not funny.

JOY. It's not a joke. I'm desperate. I could give that baby everything it would ever need. You could see it whenever you want. Think about it.

MAYA *puts on a record, 'Les Fleurs' by Minnie Riperton, downs a glass of prosecco and exits. An upstage room is revealed – it is Mum's bedroom, preserved, full of her things. SAGE appears in Mum's room with a cake. No one else turns up. YOUNG GRANNY enters to look up at SAGE. As SAGE blows out the candles on the cake, GRANNY opens the door for the MUMS in red dresses. The MUMS enter.*

They do all sorts of ordinary, unspectacular things: they call someone on the phone, hoover, read a book, roll a cigarette, dance. They live.

'Les Fleurs' builds into a dance. The song cracks and mingles with grand classical music. SAGE *smells and hugs her mum's pillow. At the climax of the dance,* SAGE *starts to rip the room apart, throwing things, pulling down a poster of John Lennon. Finally,* SAGE *rips Mum's red dress. All exit apart from* STORM. *Door closes.*

'Symphony No. 83 in G-Minor, Hob 1:83 "La paule": I. Allegro spiritoso' by Franz Joseph Haydn plays, as night turns into morning.

Chapter Seven – Morning – So Now Then…

STORM *is sat at the table, unblinking.* LUKE *enters.*

LUKE. Morning.

STORM. How did you sleep?

LUKE. Fine. You?

STORM. I'm sorry for not inviting you.

LUKE. It's okay.

STORM. I've done something terrible.

LUKE. Okay.

JOY *and* DERREN *enter.*

DERREN. Bloody hell, that bed is awful. Who wants coffee?

No answer.

I'll make a pot.

DERREN *leaves.*

JOY. I've done something terrible.

STORM. Me too.

SAGE *enters. Looks at* STORM.

SAGE. Morning, everyone.

Everyone looks at STORM.

LUKE. Storm, have you been sat here all night?

STORM. Yes. Yes I have.

MAYA *enters.*

MAYA. Gooood morning! Has anyone seen Dodo?

STORM. He went to get some croissants.

MAYA. Oh okay. So I was thinking a lot last night /

JOY. Maya, could I just borrow you /

MAYA. Joy, it's okay. I was thinking about Storm's presentation. You have been really dedicated to this family, Storm. And I think if twenty per cent of all our inheritance is what you need to make a life for yourself, we should all genuinely consider it. I'm happy to give up my chunk.

STORM. Oh god.

LUKE. Yeah. Storm did more, she should get more.

JOY. Let's keep discussing the exact amount, okay, but yes, in principle. If it makes Storm happy and means we can stay as a family. Then I think it's worth it.

STORM. Oh god.

MAYA. Sage?

SAGE. ...I don't see why not.

MAYA. The Pelican daughters! And son! Sorry, Luke! The Pelican kids. All for one and one for all!

JOY/SAGE/MAYA/LUKE. Pelican! Pelican! Pelican! Pelican! Pelican!

The chanting continues. DERREN *comes back with coffee.* DODO *enters. The chanting continues.*

DODO. Can everybody stop one second!

They stop.

MAYA. Hi.

DODO. Hi good morning. I have something that I would like to say to you all, and I would like you to take it in the spirit of honesty and forgiveness.

Maya, Dodo checking in.

MAYA. Maya checking in.

DODO. So last night, Storm and I, we fucked. It happened.

STORM. Jesus.

DODO. I'm sorry, I'm so sorry. We were high. I love you. And I am sorry. But I've been walking around all night thinking about it and I've worked it out.

This house is poison. Your sisters are poison. And Bristol is a horrible city.

Since the moment I've got here, you've all treated me like I'm some kind of joke. Well, guess what? Not any more.

Maya, we have got to get out of here. Back on the road. Where we can start a family, a real family, a better family, which communicates clearly, and tells the truth.

You keep talking about your mom like she was some kind of hero, like she gave you some special powers to live in some profound new way. But look at all of you.

Joy, you're completely joyless.

Storm, you're obsessed with money, like it's going to fix all your problems, well, guess what? It's not gonna.

Sage, you are rude and self-centred, and I've seen your website, and your art is derivative and mediocre at best.

Derren, you're alright.

Luke, I don't know you very well so I'm sorry, but you do not seem like a very nice little boy.

And your mom, God rest her soul, seems like she was one crazy, manipulative bitch! The only person in your family who seems like they have a single shred of rational thought is Grandma and I'm pretty sure she's got dementia.

Maya. Come on. Let's get out of here.

JOY. Imagine if Mum was here, / and what she'd say.

DODO. Shut up. Imagine, imagine, imagine. Shut up. Has it crossed your narrow little mind that we might not want to hear about your mom twenty-four seven?

MAYA. Don't talk to my sister like that.

DODO. Maya, We don't need them! C'mon.

He takes a step towards here. She flinches. She shakes her head.

Fine. Great. Fantastic. Thank you all for your beautiful hospitality. Dodo checking out.

JOY. Peace and love, Dodo.

He turns to her violently.

DODO. Peace and love to you too, Joy!

DODO *leaves. Silence.*

STORM. Maya, I /

MAYA. Sooo. Next on the agenda. Joy, I've had some time to consider your offer.

JOY. No, Maya. I was drunk, / it was stupid.

MAYA. You're right. My life *doesn't* have to change. I can't quite go sandboarding with a baby now, can I? I can't be a mum.

JOY. Of course you can.

DERREN. What's happening?

MAYA. I accept. You can buy my spawn! Fifty grand right? As soon as it's ready, it's yours. Of course we'll need to work out the details. I think I'll use my cut to make sure I never see any of you ever again.

DERREN. What did you do?

JOY. I know it sounds crazy but /

DERREN. You can't make those kind of decisions for us.

JOY. I didn't make the decision.

MAYA. Oh, I think we have, Derren.

JOY. Be quiet.

MAYA. I'm pretty happy with the arrangement. Fifty grand from you, fifty grand from the house – no baby. Sounds great.

DERREN. We're not buying Maya's baby!

JOY. Well, I'm considering it. I am.

Silence.

DERREN *goes to leave.*

Derren, please.

He exits.

Silence.

SAGE *starts laughing.*

She laughs and laughs and laughs.

SAGE. You're all fucking terrible people.

JOY. Right, you've ruined my life.

STORM. You're a selfish bitch.

MAYA. Oh you can talk, moneybags.

JOY. Yeah. I really hate all of you.

MAYA. The sight of you makes me want to be sick.

STORM. The feeling is mutual, Maya.

SAGE. You're all fucking terrible people. And you know what, I hate Joy the most.

JOY. Well, I think you're a cunt.

SAGE. Bring it, bitch.

STORM. You're the biggest cunt of all.

MAYA. Can we please stop using the word cunt as an insult!

STORM. Oh shut up, you self-righteous cunt.

JOY. Cunt Cunt Cunt Cunt Cunt Cunt Cunt.

SAGE. Oh fuck off.

> LUKE *leaves. They all start hurling insults at each other until it becomes a scream-off. They are just yelling incoherently.* LUKE *re-enters in Mum's dress, slams his hands on the table. They shut up.*

LUKE. No! Not in my house. No daughters of mine are going to speak to each other like that, not under this roof. If you want to discuss something. You discuss it. Calmly and constructively. We are Pelicans. We are better than this.

> *Sings.*

> 'Our blood is thick'

JOY. Luke, come on.

LUKE. 'Our blood is thick'

MAYA/STORM/JOY/SAGE. 'Our blood is thick'

LUKE. 'Thicker than hate'

MAYA/STORM/JOY/SAGE. 'Thicker than hate'

LUKE. 'Thicker than greed'

MAYA/STORM/JOY/SAGE. 'Thicker than greed'

LUKE. 'It is strong'

MAYA/STORM/JOY/SAGE. 'It is strong'

LUKE. 'Because it's bound with love. Squawk squawk.'

MAYA/STORM/JOY/SAGE. 'Because it's bound with love. Squawk squawk.'

LUKE. Good. Now apologise.

STORM. Sorry.

MAYA. Sorry.

JOY. Sorry.

SAGE. Sorry.

LUKE. Thank you. Now we are going to sit and we are going to eat our breakfast in peace.

The doorbell rings. STORM *answers.*

SOLICITOR. Hello. I'm Susie Stephens of Stephen Stephens and Sons Solicitors. I'm your solicitor. Storm, we spoke on the phone.

STORM. This isn't a good time, sorry.

SOLICITOR. Well, as I am quite busy and as this was our booked appointment, I'll dive right in if that's okay.

As you may well be aware, your mother remortgaged this property in 2005.

This mortgage was then sold by Nationwide to Santander in 2006 as a 'stated income, verified assets' mortgage and then, in June of 2009, a majority stake of fifty-one per cent of that mortgage was sold by Santander to a bank in Greece called the Patria Bank as a 'no income, verified asset' loan.

In the ten or so years that followed, the interest rates on the financial agreements through which your mortgage was divided and traded, called mortgage-backed securities, which derive their value from outlay of conflated mortgage conglomerates, have remained relatively stable.

Such financial innovations have enabled investors such as Richard Branson, Elon Musk, ExxonMobil and Berkshire

Hathaway to invest indirectly in your mortgage, and millions of others like it.

Unfortunately, due to unforeseen circumstances between EU and UK financial sectors, some of these investors and the banks and funds that they represent, have attempted to sell mortgages such as yours to other international mortgage brokers. But, as no credible buyer was found by the Patria Bank, and in an attempt to recoup lost funds, nine months ago they increased their interest rates to such an extent that they now technically own one hundred and twelve per cent of your house, which may seem counterintuitive, as it obviously isn't physically possible to own more than one hundred per cent of a house, but unfortunately it is both legally and financially very possible, and is now legally and financially a very real situation.

The SIBLINGS *begin to sit down, pour coffee, fetch bowls, spoons and cornflakes.*

I initially thought that your mother's savings might be able to cover this deficit, and leave you each with a four-figure inheritance to walk away with, but looking more closely into the numbers, your mother left just under twenty-seven thousand pounds of savings and assets which, after inheritance tax and probate fees, leaves about eighteen thousand pounds.

However, two days ago, I was contacted by Tony Cameron Lifecare PLC, and because of your grandmother's increased care needs in Tulip Manor Trust, over the last twelve months, they've retro-actively billed you for having to arrange a private residential-care package, at an additional cost of two thousand, six hundred pounds per month, as well as a one-off fee of five thousand pounds for the use of the on-site residential, nursing and dementia care home, which is also operated by Tony Cameron Lifecare PLC.

Which means, in short, that all things considered, after all taxes and fees are accounted for, including my own soliciting fee, there will be just under two hundred pounds left, and if

you don't sell this house by Friday you will immediately
default on your mortgage repayments, and that two hundred
pounds will very quickly turn into a hefty debt of several
tens of thousands of pounds.

Additionally, if you'd like me to stay here today to advise
you any further, my minimum consulting session is the one-
hour package, and my hourly rate is a hundred and
twenty-five pounds, which would leave you with roughly
seventy-one pounds.

Projection: '£71'.

I can give you five minutes now to discuss your course of
action, while I take a brief stroll outside, and then you must
let me know, by 10.15 a.m., whether or not you'd like to
retain my advisory services or not.

Thank you, I'll be back in... four minutes.

SOLICITOR *leaves.* LUKE *exits and re-enters with*
GRANNY. *'Damaged Goods' by Gang of Four plays.*
Everyone sits and eats their breakfast.

End of play.

An Intergenerational Workshop

Following the cancellation of the 2020 tour of *The Last of the Pelican Daughters* due to COVID-19, The Wardrobe Ensemble designed and published the following intergenerational workshop pack as a downloadable resource.

Hello there,

Thank you for taking the time to read this pack during these strange and tumultuous times. In different circumstances we would all be standing in a circle looking at each other face to face but, alas, we must find other ways of engaging with one another.

To give you an insight into why we wanted to put together a pack of this nature, it might be helpful to tell you a bit about the show. For those who haven't seen it, *The Last of the Pelican Daughters* revolves around four sisters who return to the family home a year after the death of their mother, Rosemary Pelican, in order to decide what to do with the house. We see a group of people grapple with notions of inheritance, loss and justice. We see a family filled with undying love for one another, while at the same time, tearing each other apart.

This project has been a labour of love for us. It began with a focus on the notion of family and inheritance and it has largely stayed true to that initial intention. However, it quickly became apparent that, when making a show about family, there was so much that could be said and so many themes to explore: inheritance, money, grief, loss, entitlement, the difference between generations, politics, to name a few.

We could see that this show could spark conversations that extended far beyond the idea of 'family' and, to put it bluntly, we had unfinished business: there's only so much ground you can cover in a ninety-minute show. We wanted to keep having these conversations, and we wanted to have them with more people.

And this is how The Intergenerational Sessions were born. Originally conceived as a series of group workshops to run alongside our tour, our intention was to enable discussion, whilst gathering material – songs, stories, opinions – that would feed into an exhibition that would grow as the tour progressed.

We held one session in Northampton, with around thirty participants aged between 19 and 75. We drew portraits of each other, built houses together, drank tea and ate cake. We discussed music, politics and our hopes for the future. We challenged each other's assumptions and found that we had a lot in common. It was an amazing afternoon, and we couldn't wait to do more.

Then COVID-19 arrived. We couldn't continue the sessions as we'd planned, but the small discoveries we made in Northampton felt more important than ever.

So we put our heads together, and here's the result. This pack is a chance for you to think through and discuss some of the themes of the show. But more importantly, it's a chance for you to engage, connect, inspire and comfort each other in uncertain times.

If this workshop manages to provoke a few conversations that otherwise wouldn't have happened, we'll be thrilled. We hope you like it.

The Wardrobe Ensemble x

The Workshop

This workshop is to be done between yourself and someone of a different generation. It could be someone you live with, a family member you are unable to see in person or someone you aren't related to and haven't even met yet. We would love to bring together as many strangers of different generations as possible, so if you would like us to connect you with someone new, please let us know by emailing emily@thewardrobeensemble.com

This workshop aims to generate conversations. You and your partner do not have to stick to the plan if you don't want to. If the conversation goes off in a new direction and you completely abandon the tasks, that's fine. If it doesn't, that's fine too. Similarly, the workshop should take roughly ninety minutes if done in one sitting, but you may find you want to break it up and complete it over a longer period of time. It's up to you.

You may also find different ways of connecting with your partner, other than those suggested here. We will lay out each task with suggestions and you can implement them in whatever way suits your method of communication.

Setting Up Your Workshop

For those of you who will be working with someone you have never met, we will share your details with your partner and agree a mode of communication with you both. That might be a phone call, email exchange or Skype/Zoom. For those who know their partner – we will leave this up to you to organise.

So you're ready to go, make sure you've set up your chosen method.

For phone calls – Have your partner's number to hand and a good phone signal. You should go through the workshop one task at a time.

For email exchanges – You can write all your answers to the workshop in one go and then send them to your partner, or do one task at a time and email back and forth.

For Skype/Zoom – Make sure you have downloaded the appropriate software and have your partner as a contact, so you're ready to call. You should go through the workshop one task at a time.

What You Will Need

- Paper and pen.
- Colouring pencils/pens (optional).
- There will be one Google form to open.

Introduce Yourselves

On whatever platform you're using, write/say your full name; something you really like; something you really dislike; something that is unique/special about you. *e.g. 'My name is Sandra Julie Johnson; I really like climbing trees; I really dislike sweaty feet; something special about me is that I can do five backflips in a row.'*

Share these with each other. This should only take five minutes.

Draw Each Other

Take it in turns to describe what you look like to your partner. *e.g. 'I have big brown eyes, a small nose, a small scar under my left eyebrow from when I tripped over my own foot and fell in a bush.'*

Based *only* on what you say about yourself, your partner must draw you. Feel free to ask each other questions.

Don't worry if you think the drawing is bad, don't be offended, it's just a bit of fun. It's interesting to hear how someone feels about what they look like.

Delivery suggestions

For phone calls or email exchanges – Take a picture on your smartphone or camera and send it via email after the workshop. If you don't have either of these devices, perhaps you could post it?

For Skype/Zoom – Reveal your picture to the camera when both of you have finished drawing.

If none of these options work for you, then you can just use your brilliant imagination.

Nature

What can you see out of your window right now? Has it changed over the last few decades, years, months, weeks?

Share your answers with your partner.

Food

Have you learnt anything new to cook while you've been self-isolating? What is your favourite recipe to cook? Could you share this with someone in the next few weeks?

Share your answers with your partner.

Build a House

Our play is set in the Pelican's family house. It is a place filled with memories and experiences that are unique to this family. We want you to create your own house together.

Think about a house that feels like home to you. What is it about this place that feels special or homely?

As a pair, you must build a house for you both to live in by deciding on its features and using the questions below. Feel free to draw your house or just talk about it.

1. What kind of house is it? An apartment block? A detached house?
2. What colour is it?
3. What are the windows like?
4. What kind of doors does it have?
5. How many rooms does it have?
6. Is there a garden or outside space?
7. What's special about this house?
8. Where's the best place to play Hide and Seek in this house?
9. What's your favourite thing about this house?

This is Your Life

Think of three turning points in your life. These are moments when your journey took a different direction. These could be big or small moments.

Share these with your partner. Was it easy or hard? Do you think about these moments often or not?

Questions

Read over the questions and statements. Choose one from the list and write/say your response to your partner.

Swap over. Your partner must choose a new question/statement.

Choose as many as you'd like; you don't have to choose them all.

1. If I could change something about myself it would be…
2. I would describe my character as…
3. I wish I could…
4. The biggest challenge I'm facing at the moment is…
5. My biggest achievement is…
6. I'm scared of…
7. Do you consider where you live now as home?
8. Is it possible to have more than one home?
9. How has your home changed?
10. The house I grew up in was…
11. Do you have the right to own your own house?
12. What is your most valuable asset?
13. What does 'being rich' mean to you?
14. Are you rich?
15. What is the most expensive item you've ever bought?
16. What have you inherited from your parents/carers?
17. I would describe my role in my family as…
18. My children are… *or* My parents are…
19. My siblings are…
20. Is it a human right to have a child?
21. It is selfish to have more than two children.
22. Are you a grown-up?

23. It's selfish to put a parent in a care home.
24. People are living too long. It's a drain on resources.
25. People under 30 are more disadvantaged than they have ever been.
26. How are you different now to ten years ago?
27. What do you think about the generation below you?
28. Technology has stopped the younger generation from communicating properly.
29. Would you like to live in a different time?
30. Where do you hope to be in ten years' time?
31. If you could live forever, would you?
32. Are you scared of dying?
33. Looking to the future, I hope...
34. What is your earliest memory?
35. I would like to be remembered as...

Music

Music plays a big part in the show and is centred around Rosemary Pelican's record collection. The sisters use the records to console themselves, to cheer each other up, and ultimately to help them remember their mother.

What song reminds you of home or family and why? What is it about that song that chimes with you?

Discuss with your partner. You might want to listen to the song together, or make a playlist of favourite songs together.

Timeline

Visit the Google form and answer the questions:
forms.gle/UJEwkWPtNr4okV697

If it's easier for one person to open the document, that person can ask their partner the questions and put their answers into the form as well as their own.

Discussion Time

What's one thing that surprised you or particularly interested you during your conversation? Feel free to discuss anything that came up for you during this workshop.

The conversation you've just had is for you and your partner.

However, if either of you want to share any aspect of your conversation or creations with us, we'd love to see what you've been up to. You might feel inspired to write or draw something after your workshop and we'd love to see that too. Send us an email to thewardrobeensemble@gmail.com or via any of our social media channels (see our website: thewardrobeensemble.com).

Thank You...

...for joining in our virtual workshop. We hope you enjoyed it. Look after yourself in these turbulent times and we hope to meet you, in person, soon.

Lots of love,

The Wardrobe Ensemble Family x

Complicité

Founded in 1983, Complicité is an international theatre company based in London led by Co-Founder and Artistic Director Simon McBurney (OBE). Complicité works across art forms, believing theatre, opera, film, installation, publication, radio, community art, social media and the internet can all be sites for this collective act of imagination.

Complicité's recent work includes *The Encounter*, *Beware of Pity*, *The Master and Margarita*, *Shun-kin* and *A Disappearing Number*. The Company also runs an award-winning Creative Learning and Participation programme, and supports artists through the Complicité Associates and 'Developed with Complicité' strands. The Company has won over fifty major theatre awards worldwide.

'Complicité's vision – to create work that strengthens human interconnection, using the complicity between the performer and the audience that is at the heart of the theatrical experience – has never been more urgent at this time where violent division has become the norm.

We live in a moment of unprecedented, sometimes brutal and ever-accelerating change. Pushing the limits of artistic experiment, which has always been key to the Company's vision, is a vital tool in unlocking the most urgent and crucial questions of our times, challenging and excavating conventional accepted norms.'

Simon McBurney, 2019

For more information on the Company's work please contact email@complicite.org

Complicite.org
Twitter: @Complicite   *YouTube*: Complicite
Facebook: /TheatredeComplicite   *Instagram*: Complicitetheatre

Registered Charity No. 1012507

ROYAL & DERNGATE NORTHAMPTON

Chief Executive Jo Gordon
Artistic Director James Dacre

Royal & Derngate Northampton is the main venue for arts and entertainment in Northamptonshire, with attendances for live events and films numbering 358,000 last year, and an additional 119,000 seeing its work on tour at over 100 venues. Named Regional Theatre of the Year in The Stage Awards in 2011 (and nominated again in 2016), the theatre won the UK Theatre Awards for Best Presentation of Touring Theatre in 2015 and Best Touring Production in 2016 for *The Herbal Bed*, and The Stage Ensemble Award and a Fringe First for *Education, Education, Education* in 2017. In 2019, Royal & Derngate was nominated for the UK Theatre 'Excellence in Inclusivity' Award and in 2020 the venue received Olivier Award nominations for *Our Lady of Kibeho* and *The Worst Witch* and saw its original commission *The Pope* adapted into *The Two Popes* by Netflix, which received an Oscar nomination for Best Adapted Screenplay.

Alongside touring nationally and internationally Royal & Derngate's Made in Northampton productions have transferred to the West End and Broadway as well as Shakespeare's Globe, the National Theatre, the Southbank Centre and the Lyric Hammersmith. In 2019, productions of *Education, Education, Education*, *The Worst Witch*, *Our Lady of Kibeho*, *Touching the Void* and *The Selfish Giant* transferred to the West End.

The venue also presents a diverse range of visiting productions on both the Derngate and Royal stages, featuring musicals, dance, comedy and music, including a residency from the Royal Philharmonic Orchestra. Last year the venue hosted the UK Musical Theatre Conference, Devoted & Disgruntled 14 and the International Teach First conference.

Royal & Derngate's award-winning, nationally recognised Get Involved programme engages with over 20,000 participants each year, including schools, families and communities in Northamptonshire and beyond, and its two-screen cinema welcomed over 78,000 audience members to the best in world, independent, British and mainstream film. Meanwhile, the theatre's Generate artistic-development programme supports hundreds of local and emerging artists and practitioners each year. Royal & Derngate also continues to work in partnership to manage The Core at Corby Cube.

www.royalandderngate.co.uk
Facebook: /royalandderngate
Twitter: @royalderngate

www.nickhernbooks.co.uk

facebook.com/nickhernbooks

twitter.com/nickhernbooks